D1374256

Dan Pearson

is an influential landscape and garden designer with an international reputation for design and planting excellence. Dan trained at RHS Garden Wisley and the Royal Botanic Gardens, Kew, before starting his professional career as a designer in 1987.

Dan Pearson Studio, his London-based practice, handles a wide range of projects internationally for private and public clients comprising private gardens, public spaces, architectural landscaping, public parks and civic plantings. Design projects include Althorp House, the Millennium Dome, the London Maggie's Centre, Evelina Children's Hospital, RIBA, Broughton Hall, Roppongi Hills and Tokachi Millennium Forest, as well as a variety of gardens and landscapes designed for private clients.

Dan Pearson is the weekly gardening columnist for *The Observer Magazine*, co-author with Sir Terence Conran of *The Essential Garden Book* (Conran Octopus), and author of *Spirit: Garden Inspiration* (FUEL) and *The Garden: A Year At Home Farm* (Ebury Press), which was also a six part BBC TV series. He has presented and appeared in TV series on BBC2, Channel 4 and Channel 5 and has designed five award-winning Chelsea Flower Show gardens. Dan is also a Tree Ambassador for the British Tree Council. www.danpearsonstudio.com

Howard Sooley

is a photographer originally from Yorkshire, now based in London. His work has been exhibited in solo and group shows in Britain, Europe and Japan.

He has contributed to many magazines around the world including, *The Observer Magazine*, *Vogue*, *House & Garden* and *Gardens Illustrated*. Publications include *Derek Jarman's Garden* (Thames & Hudson), *Family: Photographers Photograph Their Families* (Phaidon), and *Gardener Cook* (Francis Lincoln). www.howardsooley.com

Home Ground: Sanctuary in the City

PHOTOGRAPHY BY HOWARD SOOLEY

Dan Pearson Home Ground: Sanctuary in the City

Contents

11   FOREWORD BY

HOWARD SOOLEY

Introduction

17   THE BEGINNING

19   THE OLD GARDEN

22   OASIS

24   SOIL

34   THE DESIGN

37   TREES

40   TOOLS

Winter

57   BEAUTY IN THE WRECKAGE

59   RIGHT PLANT, RIGHT PLACE

60   PLANTING

62   EVERGREEN

64   FRONT GARDEN

75   SCENT

78   HAMAMELIS

80   WINTER PRUNING

90   CLEAR-UP

92   GROUND COVER

94   'BRAZEN HUSSY'

95   SPRING SOWING

97   HELLEBORES AND SNOWDROPS

Spring

107 MULCH AND WEEDING

109 SPRING BULBS

112 LIGHT

121 TULIPS

123 CONTROL

124 WISTERIA

126 EPIMEDIUM

128 SPRING FLOWERS

140 FOLIAGE

144 VEGETABLES

154 ROSES

158 POTTING-ON

159 BAMBOO

169 IRIS

Summer

177 COMBINATIONS

179 SOLSTICE

180 LILIES

183 ZENITH

193 HEMEROCALLIS

196 ECOSYSTEM

199 TRANSPARENCY

218 PELARGONIUM

220 CLIMBERS

Autumn

229 PERSICARIA

231 PLANTING BULBS

241 HARVEST

243 SEED-SAVING

244 LATE-FLOWERING BULBS

246 PROPAGATION

257 CHANGES

259 PREPARING FOR WINTER

270 GARDEN PLAN

Foreword by Howard Sooley

I have visited Dan and Huw's garden many times over the past four years, at all times of the year, all times of the day and in all weathers. The garden is surrounded by a dizzying urban sprawl, street after street of Edwardian and Victorian houses punctuated by the occasional tower block and small parade of shops, where concrete-footed plane trees slowly count out time to the rumble and blur of red buses, scurrying feet and piercing sirens.

I love city gardens – they help us hear the distant whisper of nature, and show us the seasons coming and going, which have almost been drowned out by the city. This is an unusual garden for an urban setting, it is not reliant on solid structure for its staging, there is nowhere for nature to hide or to be obscured. It is constantly laid bare and at work before you. It is a place where time never stands still, it ebbs and flows, moving in and out like the tide, washing up against the fences, spilling through the soil and flooding over paths.

In winter the garden is unusually empty. It is at low tide, flat and motionless, under big open south London skies. This openness lets the sky in right down to the dark earth, to light the pale, broken skeletons of the *Eryngiums* or the frost-scythed perennials being swallowed back into the soil.

In spring, green seeps through the soil and on into summer, always moving, the garden swells and swirls and spills with colour. It is an orchestrated wilderness of an imaginary landscape.

For my part in this book, I wanted to try and show this garden as it changes throughout the seasons, and share some of the things I have seen on my many visits. Freeze the movement for a moment; hold the glimpse through the flowers and arching stems to see the space, colour and texture. See the flatness of winter's void for its importance and beauty, and in the height of summer show the intricate and delicate form in the apparent chaos of exuberance.

For me, this is an extraordinary urban garden, where no attempt is made to own nature. Instead it has helped me reconnect to nature. I shall miss the frequency of my trips there and remember the kindness and hospitality of Dan and Huw.

PAGES 2–3
The sky above the garden at 10 p.m. on a midsummer's evening.

PAGES 6–7
Black bamboo stems.

PAGE 10
Bamboo and wisteria shadows on the living room wall.

Introduction

The Beginning

1997 was a year that presented change. I had been working hard, without any conception of the number of directions in which I was being pulled, and I had no idea how much I needed ground under my feet again. I had completed a book that summer, was writing a weekly column for the *Sunday Times* and was curating an exhibition at the Design Museum. My design business was still small at that point but I had taken on a studio in which my assistant and I were rattling around with just enough furniture, a drawing board and a solitary computer. Earlier that summer I had completed a third TV series for Channel 4, which had taken me more than once to the States and twice to Japan. When I came off my bike in the September and broke my arm, a friend said that a metaphorical hand had reached out and said, 'Stop!'. She was right and I came to a halt or, I realize now, to the end of one chapter and the beginning of the next.

I had moved to London in 1991 and had been living three storeys up in a one-bedroom apartment in Vauxhall. Until then, life had been grounded by gardening, but the six years in Bonnington Square had drawn me into another way of living. It was a lot of fun being part of the square, where everyone had pulled together to live in the city in a different way. Central to that was the community garden we made in a disused lot where seven houses had been bombed in the war. It was a place that drew people together but, although we put heart and soul into it, the garden was a shared space that necessarily demanded that I kept a degree of distance. I looked down on it from the roof garden,

PAGES 14–15
Evaluating a late summer edit of the garden.

PAGE 16
A bowl of poppy seedheads.

which occupied the flat roof above my kitchen. I loved this little eyrie, and it was the first real garden that I could call my own, but each year it felt as if it was getting smaller as I began to pine for soil under my feet.

Chance had brought me to the heart of London, and I hadn't expected to be doing less and less of what I loved. Designing gardens and writing and talking about them had pulled me away from the simple act of getting my hands dirty. However, I was fortunate to be able to escape the city to do just that at Home Farm in Northamptonshire. This was the third garden I had made with Frances Mossman, who was the perfect client, giving me the room to work and to think. During the fourteen years I worked at Home Farm, she also encouraged me to treat the garden as my own.

I travelled there monthly to get my fix, working intensely for three days at a stretch and learning to cut my cloth on a big scale. But when I got in the car to drive home after each immersion, I knew I would have to live with the garden only in my mind until the next time. That was hard because gardens change every day, in a series of moments never to be repeated. These were moments missed, which left me hankering for a more constant relationship with a garden. It sounds slightly ungrateful to write it down and, to the contrary, I loved my borrowed garden and the land at Home Farm. I just missed being able to put a spade in the earth with the knowledge that I was investing in my own ground. Meanwhile, on my rooftop garden, I had the increasing feeling that I wasn't gardening for real. The garden was unable to put its roots down and was, like me, straining at the leash.

My partner Huw and I had started looking to move, but we had failed to find somewhere with a garden that was large enough. Living so centrally had spoiled us, and when the house in Peckham came up for sale, we imagined that it would be too far from the centre of London, that we would feel isolated without the Tube and would miss the proximity of the river. Surely the whole point of living in town was that you could move around it with ease and really feel a part of it? However, all those things were of little consequence the day we walked into the next chapter.

It was late September and the lime tree that was buckling the railings at the front of the house was already dropping its foliage. The ground, steps and windowsills were blackened by the honeydew that had rained down from its branches, while an ivy that the vendor had decapitated was browned and clinging to the walls. The paint was peeling, the windows were filthy, and inside a greasy tidal mark illustrated the passage of a large dog down the hallway. The house had been divided into bedsits, and each room was a different colour as students had made the house their own. The back windows were rotten and the walls were streaming where rain was coming in at the top of the house. There was a distinct smell of neglect, but it had the bones of a good house and I knew it was ours the moment the sliding doors were pulled back and I stepped into the garden.

The afternoon light was streaming in through autumnal trees at the end, and I strode into the damp clearing that was the remains of a lawn. The gardens to either side of the house ran uphill to the left and down to the right. There were trees as a backdrop, and a swell of vegetation between the two rows of houses that you could smell made the air sweeter. Brambles blurred the boundaries and gave way to clattering blackbirds as I pushed my way to the end. As I swung around, lost in the excitement, my hands stinging from nettles and my trousers dampened by the undergrowth, I found the house standing some distance away. A blank canvas lay between us and I didn't give it a second thought that this was home ground. A month later, Huw and I had moved in.

The Old Garden

Immediately outside the sliding doors from the basement was a tiny patio with a set of slippery steps up to the next level. You had to squeeze past an overgrown fuchsia to rise up a metre onto a terrace of concrete slabs that ran alongside the extension in the shade. As far as we could gather, the extension had been built in the 1970s and it blocked the sun up by the house. There were the remains of a carefully planted garden. The fuchsia was a white *Fuchsia magellanica*, and a leapfrogging *Clerodendrum bungei* was pushing through the clearing that had been the lawn. Jasmine and brambles wound around the steps up to the extension, the brambles forming an almost impenetrable barrier at the far side of the clearing. Rising up to the right was an ancient pear tree that had been dead for some time, and there were fruiting bodies of honey fungus at its feet. If you leaned on the trunk, it creaked against a rotting larch lap fence, and it was hard to tell if the tree supported the fence or the fence the tree. As I made my way up the garden, I spotted *Rosa* 'Mermaid', a white buddleia and drifts of *Cyclamen hederifolium* among the undergrowth.

Throwing shade onto the tangle of grass was an enormous *Cytisus battandieri* with wide outstretched limbs and a gnarled fist of a root bowl. The brambles were lacing the branches and overwhelming the fruit trees beyond. Pushing through the thicket towards an unwieldy

PAGES 20–1
The garden in November 1997.
Top left: Looking back towards the house.
Bottom left: The sunken terrace.
Top right: The end of the garden.
Bottom right: View down the garden.

20

and clearly vigorous weeping willow, there was a second clearing formed by the shade of the willow and its branches. They lashed across the ground when the wind blew scoring marks in the mud. Closer in, under the tumble of nettles and deadly nightshade, were burned-out incinerators and wheelbarrows with punctures. These were the remains of a garden that had, for the best part of a decade, been allowed to run to rack and ruin.

We moved in during November and, as the winter came upon us and the leaves eventually fell from the undergrowth, we began to see the old footprint. A perimeter path framed the end of the garden, and a twisted eucalyptus, more in our neighbour's garden than ours, had broken the fence at the end. There were compost heaps, too, brick-built in the angle between the end wall and the garages to the left. These were one of the better finds, as was the soil. I had taken my spade with me that first day and plunged it in at several points across the garden. The soil remained deep and dark and uninterrupted by rubble piles or air-raid shelters or the concrete footings of long-gone garden sheds. It represented potential, and every bone in my body felt right about being there.

Oasis

Although the roof terrace in Vauxhall was small, just four by five metres, it allowed me to live out in the open in the centre of the city and to be in touch with the sky, the seasons and the elements. It was designed with the London skyline as a backdrop, and creating a strong sense of place was key to the surprise as you climbed the stairs to the door onto the roof. The materials took their lead from the surrounding slate roofs, the leading and chimneypots, while the planting was designed to capture the wind and light, celebrating the location three floors up. As an extension to the tiny apartment, the roof garden was a sanctuary and remained as one until the need to get soil under my feet again prompted the move to the garden here.

Identifying a sense of place is key to all of my work and it is what I tune into as the starting point from which the direction of a garden takes its lead. I made an exception here, in order to create a mood that worked against the buzz of the surrounding city. Central to my thinking was the idea of the oasis. I wanted to create somewhere that was an antidote to the hustle and bustle, the hard edges and the sheer number of people competing for space at ground level. True,

I 'borrowed' my neighbours' trees to help me build this tranquil place but, within the walls and fences, I created my own set of rules.

I wanted to be able to actively garden here rather than simply tend a garden. Gardening is a process, and the best parts of it are in the doing and the immediate engagement. I have gardened since I was five or six and feel lucky to have found that passion so young. I completely subscribe to the theory that the activity you loved doing most as a child – the state of utter absorption – is the very thing you should find a way of repeating as an adult. Over time I have come to the understanding that the reason gardening makes me feel so grounded is that it brings together the physical and the cerebral and acts as a form of meditation.

It has been a demanding brief for the garden in Peckham to be all the things that I need it to be while retaining serenity. As an environment, it has to offer considerably more than a merely aesthetic experience – I need to be able to experiment and continue to learn about my raw materials. A garden should never be static and there has to be room for it to shift and to change. I want nature, or a version of it, to be present here and I want the seasons to be mapped in the hardened heart of the city. The garden provides for me as I also grow food to eat, and I can gather a posy every day of the year, which allows me to live with my plants up close. The balance is never fixed, in that the garden is always changing and demanding my attention to keep it in balance, but this is the reason I do it and it keeps things feeling vital.

Although London is an energizing place to live, I want to be transported somewhere entirely more restful once I step into the garden. The first thing you do when you open the back door (and friends and family immediately remark on this, too) is breathe out and exhale. The surroundings make the next breath in taste so much better. I believe that the greenery makes the air sweeter here and that the mood in the garden puts you in a better frame of mind. It is a sensual place that encourages you to brush the felt-leaved *Pelargonium* as you move from the house, to gaze at the sky or watch the rain rippling the surface of the water bowl beneath the *Cercis*. The breeze in the bamboos baffles the city hubbub, the shadow patterns play with the light, and you can smell the damp and the rot on the air in the autumn. It is a place that has its own life and its own rhythms. Winter has its beginning, its middle and its end. When the garden strains towards and then tips beyond the longest day into the second half of the summer, I can feel it in the planting. I spend as much time as possible living outside because the garden draws me there. It is the first place I go after getting out of bed and the last at the end of the day.

Soil

Not so long ago, before these houses were erected, the land around here was used as kitchen gardens. Before that, the open ground supported willow beds for the production of withies for basket making. It is just two miles to the Thames and I guess that, on occasion, the flood plain may have extended this far. The soil gives something of this away, with river-washed pebbles in a deep alluvial loam. Dig down a spit or so and you find clay. It is what you might describe as hearty soil – never so heavy as to be waterlogged, nor so light that it dries out completely in summer.

On my first viewing, before we bought the house, I came prepared with a border spade. This would be the first piece of ground that I could call my own and I remember the excitement of discovering what I might have to work with. It was clear that things grew well here since the weeds in the garden were lush, and as I plunged the blade into the remains of the lawn, the sod yielded easily. When I brought a handful to my nose, it was dark and crumbly and sweet-smelling. It felt good as I crumbled it through my fingers, still warm from the summer and moist enough to be able to squeeze into a ball. If it had been a clay loam, I would have been able to test its consistency by rolling it into a ball in my palm but, with its silt content, the topsoil crumbled to the touch. London gardens are often blighted by soil that has been ruined in the past, with basement excavations and rubble and glass buried or strewn on the nearest piece of ground. But the soil here, where I could get to it, seemed consistently good and I left on that first visit convinced that this was the place to be.

For my first two decades, I gardened on thin acidic sand, and for the third on the contrasting heavy Midlands clay at Home Farm. These are the extremes – the sand easy to work but without guts, the clay sticky but wholesome once you had improved it. The soil in Peckham promised to be easier and I gave myself a year to get to know it while I was clearing the garden. Soil is the very foundation of a garden and understanding the raw material is fundamental to the way a garden develops. Knowing how to look after your soil and putting the time into improving its potential is never time wasted.

First impressions are often misleading and, as soon as the protective layer of weeds was stripped away, the winter rains had an immediate impact. The soil had been easy to fork free from its protective covering, but the shingle in the ground came up to the surface and the ground lay sticky and unworkable with winter wet once it was exposed. I was keen to get the measure of it and see what

PAGE 25
View of the garden from the living room window.

PAGES 26–7
Cercis canadensis 'Forest Pansy' on the lower terrace.

PAGES 28–9
An October view towards the house.

PAGES 30–1
The end of the garden in October.

it could support without improvement, so I set out a vegetable patch to grow a range of plants for the following summer that would show me what the soil was made of. It was a damp June and the soil lay heavy and wet and had to be worked from boards but, as soon as the weather improved, it dried out fast. Despite the fact that one spit down the clay was holding some moisture, the dusty capping soon looked impoverished and the vegetables were only half as good as I had imagined they might be.

The truth of the matter, if you are intending to garden, is that all soil needs to be nurtured. Though not all plants need a soil rich in organic matter, the addition of compost or manure, leaf mould or even composted bark improves a soil immeasurably. Organic matter opens up a soil prone to lying wet and compacted by winter rains and helps it hold the moisture in the ground when a dry summer is upon us. It also provides the feeding ground for the all-important earthworm. A good population of earthworms is another measure of healthy soil, and encouraging them with organic matter is key. Worm burrows allow air and water to travel through the soil easily and, in the process of feeding, worms drag leaf litter from the surface and deposit it as droppings in their burrows. Worms are the silent cultivators that go on regardless as long as the environment is in balance and there is a good supply of organic matter. Although I had initially found a proliferation of earthworms in the top layer of soil where ten years of neglect and leaf litter had accumulated, as soon as this was stripped away when clearing the garden, the worms were harder to find. Improving the soil and then protecting it was a given and, at the end of the first summer and before any more planting was started, I spent a month working goodness into the ground.

Getting organic matter in bulk is easy in the country and I had been spoiled at Home Farm where there was always a pile of farmyard manure. When we ran out of manure, we ordered in a lorry load of mushroom compost, and when the suppliers cottoned on that this waste product had value and it became too expensive, we got a supply of recycled green waste from the local council. The manure was forked into newly cultivated ground, and an annual mulch of compost improved it from the surface. In five years we had turned a sticky clay into a good, retentive loam.

I knew I had a good start here in Peckham because the ground was hearty, but the soil needed organic matter to set it up for the future. Several loads of mushroom compost were deposited in tonne bags in the drive and barrowed through the garage. A finger's depth was spread over the surface and forked to the depth of a spit and that

PAGE 32
Adirondack chairs beneath the hornbeam.

was enough to set the planting up for the good start that it needed. In subsequent years, I have worked my own compost into new planting pits and the vegetable beds. When perennials retreat below ground in the winter, the organic content is topped up from time to time with mulch where the soil lies bare. I am happy that the soil is now in balance and try to disturb it as little as possible, leaving the earthworms in peace to work fallen foliage into the ground and do the bulk of the work for me.

The Design

Designing my own garden was one of the most difficult things I have ever done. There were too many plants that I wanted to grow, an endless list of possibilities, and far too many 'stories' to try to squeeze into one place. I found this crippling at first and decided to take a year to get to know the space, to inform the direction it took.

The first winter was spent clearing the undergrowth to see what the land looked like. Removing the thicket of brambles that had engulfed the central third of the garden had an enormous impact. Without the support of the briars, the fence came down in the first winter gale and opened us up to our neighbours who, fortunately, were incredibly relaxed about the two gardens being one. Our dilapidated boundary was righted again and held up in makeshift manner with guy ropes until fencing contractors replaced it.

The twisted fruit trees had been dragged down by the brambles, and a thicket of buddleia and nettles lay beyond them. An uninterrupted carpet of *Allium triquetrum* had colonized the shade at their feet and I can still smell the savoury crush of its winter foliage as I write. The fruiting bodies of honey fungus on the dead pear tree were enough of a sign to be wary of leaving too many roots in the ground and I pick-axed the bramble and dug out the roots. It took a whole weekend of axe work to shift the eucalyptus, and another to shave the filthy ivy off the garages at the end. We worked from boards, being careful not to compact the ground on the repeated trips made with the wheelbarrow. Several enormous heaps of debris were left to dry under tarps before being burned at a twilight party we held to celebrate the clearance.

The garden was reduced back to bare bones and fences. I decided to leave the willow, though I already knew that it would be too much of an influence, and I took a risk on the *Cytisus*, despite another cluster of fungus at its root. The 'Mermaid' rose was pruned and trained up the fence, and the remains of the lawn cut back with an electric hover mower given to me by a friend. I knew that the lawn was also temporary, as I could think of better things to do with my land and my time, but it was clear, clean space that allowed me to think.

I watched how the light changed as the sun moved on its axis, and repositioned a chair around the garden to see where the hot spots were and where the wind whistled between the houses. Endless cups of tea were drunk sitting on the chair imagining the garden-to-be. The bamboo hedge ultimately helped with the wind, but that was yet to come. My plants remained in pots in the shade of the *Cytisus*. It was a gathering collection as I grasped at straws.

A whole year after moving here, and several sketch plans later, work began on the landscaping. I knew I would need an ante-chamber between the house and the garden where we could live out in the open. The courtyard gardens of Japan had made an impression on me, and I wanted an unornamented space that would be quiet and reflective. There would be a table and seating here but not much more. Beyond it anything could happen, and probably would. The gardened garden would be held at bay by the terrace.

Thirty-five tonnes of soil were dug out to extend the terrace to the end of the extension. The terrace was split in two, to take up the metre's difference in level, with the lower section flush with the basement floor, and the upper level midway between that and the garden. I had found some giant slabs of a dark grey Indian limestone that were large enough to present quite a challenge in getting them through the garage. Graham, the landscaper, customized his son's skateboard to make a trolley that negotiated the distance from the lorry to the terrace. The terrace emerged from the sea of mud like the clean inside of a new cardboard box. The huge pieces of stone were laid mostly as they came, but a few were cut down so that the joints could be offset. They were left unpointed, and I planted a few pieces of mind-your-own-business to travel, moss-like, in the cracks. The limestone was dark when it went down, but over the years it has lightened considerably. On a bright day it is matte, silvery and more light-reflective than you would ever imagine a dark stone could be. When it is wet, it is dark as charcoal and shiny as granite, and I love the way it changes so dramatically with the weather.

I wanted cantilevered steps to float in the rendered walls, which I had plans to light from underneath, but I have never got around to it, although there is now a series of lights that uplights the bamboo hedge. I prefer to use lanterns further into the garden, rather than rely upon the flick of a switch to bring it to life at night.

A wooden deck and a cantilevered wooden bench form the lower level to the terrace, so that the floor of the house appears to flow through the sliding doors. I was lucky to stumble upon a giant terracotta bowl at Covent Garden flower market and this is the focal feature on the lower level. The *Cercis canadensis* has made this position its own and interrupts the view from the kitchen in the summer, so that you can never see the garden all at once. A large terracotta pan sits beneath it, which we keep filled with water, both for the reflections and for the cats to drink from. This and the copper on the far deck are the only water elements in the garden, but they are enough to bring the sky to earth and provide another layer of life. The copper is now full of water lilies.

In the middle of the garden, another deck repeats the wood of the first. It is slightly raised, like a dais, so that you step up onto it from the path. It was originally worked around the *Cytisus* (this has now been replaced by a hornbeam after honey fungus struck the pineapple broom down), and it makes a cool clearing where shadow patterns can fall on an uninterrupted surface.

I had two attempts at making a path to connect these two areas. The straight line of the first drew you too rapidly through the planting. Although I wanted the path to be like a line of desire through a meadow, the directness and speed of movement it demanded was wrong. By widening it slightly in the middle and working in the gentlest of curves, it slowed your pace so that you were encouraged to pause and ponder on the way. Two dark limestone slab benches were added to the path, one on each side, to help this feeling by acting as destinations. The bench in the sun heats up in the summer and is home to my species *Pelargonium*. I try to keep the bench in the shade empty as a resting point for contemplation but this rarely happens, as there are just too many pots.

The paths and a clearing at the end of the garden were surfaced in shards of tumbled limestone, which you are most aware of at night when you are not using your eyes so much. The pacing in the garden is interesting underfoot. I like the way you move from wood to solid stone to the clatter of broken limestone, then wood and clatter again as you move through the garden. In the summer, when the windows are open, you can hear the foxes and the cats coming and going.

The clearing at the end of the garden took a little more time to resolve itself, as I had not yet committed to removing the willow tree. For a while I maintained a pool of grass with informal beds lapping around it but, when the willow came out, so did the grass, and in came the evening light. I so enjoy the way the light collects in the garden, and its westerly aspect is, for me, the perfect one. Two raised beds for herbs and salad defined the new clearing into which I worked an area for the pots and eventually the cold frame. Last, but certainly not least, is the stepping stone path that picks its way through my special shady area to the compost heap. The paving stones are the remains of the concrete path that originally ran through the garden. Although far from special, I like the way they link one incarnation of the garden to the next.

Trees

The willow tree was a splendid thing in its way, in the first flush of youth and growing more than a metre a year in every direction. It had been planted close to the wall at the back and I'm guessing it was about twenty years old. It was already a big baby in a small pram – it reached over the boundaries, was half the width of the garden and was clearly spreading fast. Its branches swept to the ground to worry the life out of anything within reach, and on windy days it would swish its locks in a captivating performance.

In the winter, I confess I liked the way the light fell upon the cascade of lime-green branches, but it was the wrong tree for the garden. Its summer foliage was dense, so dense that, when the sun swung behind it, half the garden lost the evening light entirely. Although I tried to like it, its size and prominence set the scene and there was no getting away from its watery associations. I had also had concerned enquiries from our neighbours at the back. As well as one of their gardens being completely overwhelmed, they were both worried about willow's famous water-seeking roots damaging their drains or causing subsidence.

For two winters I battled with the idea of removing it before plucking up the courage to do so. When I explained to the tree surgeon who took it down why I wanted it gone, he said, 'You're quite a bully, aren't you?', but, in truth, that conscience-pricking moment was the worst of it once I had made my decision. When I returned from work that evening to find the space where it had been, I didn't give it a second thought. The weight of the tree was lifted and the garden was free to go in any direction.

Trees are a mixed blessing in a small garden and we are lucky to have trees around us that are borrowed as the backdrop. The elderly sycamore three gardens down is magnificent and proof that, as mature trees, they do have character. It has drama against a winter sky and is home to the crows that roost there. That said, it is far enough away for us not to be affected by its roots and the sticky honeydew that falls from the branches when the aphids are present. I do not have the bulk of autumn foliage either, and only a handful of keys makes it over the fence. The ash trees to the north are also far enough away for us to get the best of their influence. They reach up high to fray the skyline with feathery foliage and offer resting places for the birds that move through the corridors of greenery. To the south, there is nothing tall enough to prevent the sun from streaming in. Consequently, I am also free of roots and, as a result, I have options. Within reason, I can choose what I want to grow here and am in the luxurious position of being able to sacrifice some sun and make my own shade.

I would not want a garden without trees, for they lift the eye away from boundary level. Trees change the mood around them. They create cool, there is life in their branches, and their movement is always a whisper that you are happy to hear. The dappled light they throw to the ground is also something that I never tire of and, of all the plants to manifest the seasons, there are few that do it with such drama. Under their skirts you can garden with a completely different range of material, with gentle woodlanders and plants that like protection. And, here in the city, trees breathe life back into the stale, polluted air.

I miss the maturity that established trees bring to a new garden, and it was a challenge to start from scratch. With the willow tree gone and nothing more than the elderly *Cytisus* to provide a microclimate in my now empty box, I set about making a selection. This was difficult because planting a tree is an investment in time and there are few things that make it as apparent that time, your time, marches swiftly. There is no denying it, planting trees makes you aware of your mortality and it would be nice to think that there was at least another life in which you could get to know them better. If you get it wrong, which I did, you have to be philosophical and not see the mistake as time lost but as time spent getting to know something new.

Although it is easy to forget, in a decade I went through several stages to get to where we are now. In the first summer here, while the willow tree was still standing, I toyed with *Amelanchier*, intending to invite two seasons in with spring blossom and autumn foliage. I never did that because it felt too easy, but they were at the top of the list for a while. The *Genista aetnensis* that are now at the front of the house proved to be too constant and unchanging a presence in the back garden and I missed the seasonal change in their branches. I wanted something unusual and flirted with a little grove of *Betula albosinensis* var. *septentrionalis* to fray the skyline when the willow came out. I had discovered them years beforehand when working at the Edinburgh Botanic Garden and thought the coloured stems would go with the direction that the garden was taking at that stage. I also wanted trees that would do something fairly quickly without casting too much shade. I wanted everything of those trees, but the birch didn't feel right either and, within a year, they were moved to my parents' garden.

I replaced them with a group of coyote willows (*Salix exigua*), which grew fast and sent a silvery shoal of branches into the air to complement the *Cytisus*. They lived fast and died young after falling apart in their seventh year. I guess the soil was too rich for them – they live in boulder-strewn valleys on the shores of rivers in their native North America. But they were a delight while I had them and no more so than when the long-tailed tits tumbled twittering through their branches in search of aphids. This was the only time the cats have caught birds in the garden and I console myself with that thought now that the willows are gone.

The *Catalpa* x *erubescens* 'Purpurea' caught me by surprise in the nursery and I bought three within minutes of seeing them. The young foliage was darkest purple, overlaid with liquorice veining, and there was a sheen on the upper leaf that seemed to catch the blue of the early summer sky. Their stems were grey and graceful and I liked that they leafed up late and allowed spring sunshine through their branches to reach the plants awakening at ground level. As they matured, which was fast, they soon came to flower. This was when the verticillium wilt revealed itself, collapsing the growth on random branches just before the flower buds opened. I lived with it for the best part of five years, hoping each July that it wouldn't strike again, but it was relentless and unpredictable. Eventually, I tired of the trees hanging in tatters just when the garden was at its best and removed them.

For a window of three or four years, the *Catalpa* had been perfect with the *Cystisus battandieri*, but the *Cytisus* suddenly succumbed to a lingering case of honey fungus. Now I was exposed, with a problem developing in the *Catalpa*, and the maturity of the oldest plant in the garden erased in the space of a winter. I have never been one to plant mature trees, favouring the ease with which a youngster settles into new ground, but I replaced the *Cytisus* with a semi-mature, multi-stemmed hornbeam (*Carpinus*), which I rescued from my 2004 Chelsea Flower Show garden. Hornbeams are simple trees, plain and as versatile as they are disease-resistant. It took three men, a forklift and a dismantled fence to get it in from the alley at the side but, when the tree leafed up the following spring and I could stand in its shade that summer, I knew it was safe to remove the *Catalpa*.

One should never be afraid of change, particularly not in a garden setting where change is inevitable, but I have missed the *Catalpa*. They broke the linearity of the garden, and the privacy that they afforded me on the deck at the end will take some time to come back. I have not missed the wilt and I know it is lurking and waiting for a suitable host (*Catalpa* are prone). I read that the *Cornus kousa* var. *chinensis*, which has replaced them, are less susceptible and I hope this is the case. I have chosen a free-flowering form called 'China Girl' and, since this is a garden that is as much about getting-to-know as it is growing my favourite things, I am looking forward to making its acquaintance. To date, the foliage has a rather sullen look to it where it hangs in the branches but the tiers of flowering bracts are glorious and long-lived in May and June and they are my antidote for there not being blossom in the garden. I think it will like this spot, and I am now old enough to know I will have to wait to see if it is the tree for this particular position.

Tools

Good tools are a pleasure to own and, over the years, I have built up a stock of essentials. I have two of most things, although I have a favourite of each, and certain things I could not do without. Apart from my border fork (a hand-me-down from my mother, worn and delicate like a precision instrument), there is nothing particularly special about the tools in the garage. What sets them apart from the average spade and fork is that the majority are well designed and manufactured. They are well balanced, well thought out, made from good materials and nicely fashioned. At a garden centre you would find them at the top of their price range, and yet I have never once regretted the outlay. Good tools are designed to last and, with luck and good maintenance, that should be a lifetime.

That said, the plastic builder's barrows, buckets, brooms, shovel and pick were bought from the local building suppliers. They are cheap and workmanlike and made to take rough treatment. I use the barrow infrequently now that the heavy work is over, but it would take daily use. I first saw the rubber buckets in Europe, though they are common here now, and I fill them with water to plunge dessicated pots into or as day-to-day buckets for weeding or lifting. I have two and they stack, which is convenient where space is limited.

I have three Haws watering cans, which are worth the investment: two two-gallon cans and a one-gallon can, which is nimble and good when watering seedlings. The long, slender spout is the perfect

PAGE 41
Eryngium giganteum.

PAGES 42–3
The late autumn slump, with compost heaps in the far left-hand corner.

PAGES 44–5
Turning the compost heaps.

PAGES 46–7
Overwintering spring bulbs.

counterbalance to the weight of the can and makes watering an elegant exercise. I have three roses, each with a slightly different perforation, which I favour depending upon the robustness of seedlings. The roses are easy to remove and fit nicely in the palm of your free hand when you are watering without them. I have a no-frills lance with an on-off catch that I attach to the hose in the high summer, but I prefer to use the cans and keep them full so that the plants get water that is at air temperature. I'm not sure this matters with most things but it feels like it should. The hose, which I leave coiled under the hornbeam, is just long enough to extend to the pots at the end. It is green, while the hose I reel out when more length is needed is yellow, which encourages me to put it away.

I favour stainless-steel implements, as they shed the soil more easily when it is wet and sticky in the winter. They are also easier to clean when I am feeling tidy. I have two full-sized forks, two spades and a stainless-steel border fork to complement my mother's, as well as two border spades. While the standard-sized tools are good for digging on the allotment, turning the compost and planting and lifting trees and shrubs, the border tools get most frequent use, as they focus your energy down to a defined point, which matters when the garden is full to bursting.

I have a large plastic rake, which is great for gathering the bamboo leaves on the terrace, and a steel pronged rake to knock the soil to a tilth on the allotment. A stainless-steel hoe is useful there, too, but I prefer to weed with hand-tools or the border fork in the jam-packed garden. I have a selection of trowels, as they are easily lost. Another reason I prefer stainless steel is that it is reflective and easy to find. The best trowels have a long, slender blade. There is one with a sharp point so I can winkle out the tap-rooted weeds. I use the hand-forks less, but they are great for working broadcast annual seed into the surface.

I am fussy about pruning equipment, as it has to be up to the job of cutting cleanly and precisely. This requires several calibres of blade and it is imperative that they are kept in good condition. Although I have various pruning knives, it is usually the secateurs I reach for. I have four pairs because I feel lost without them and ill-equipped if I can't feel them in my back pocket. They get used for cutting string, deadheading, harvesting fruit and vegetables and general pruning. All of them are Felco No. 2, and I keep a pair in the kitchen and two on the shelf by the door in the garage. The sharpest pair is always kept in a cupboard and only brought out to prune when I need the cuts to be perfect. It is reserved for the wisteria, the roses and any woody plants. As soon as cutting becomes laboured with the sharpest pair,

PAGE 48
My Turkish knife.

a 'working' pair is sent away to be sharpened and then put in the cupboard for best to keep the rota going. This way, I never pick up a pair that is not up to the job.

I have two sets of Felco loppers, one with mid-length handles, the other with long handles for increased leverage on larger limbs. You should never force a cut and, as soon as the loppers are not up to it, I move on to a folding hand-saw with a fifteen-centimetre blade. When that is too small, a hand-saw with a thirty-centimetre blade and a longer cut usually does the job. I have a small Turkish knife with a serrated edge that is half-saw, half-knife, and is perfect for cutting back the perennials at the end of winter.

There are odds and ends in the shed that are kept in an old trug, which Frances gave me when she left Home Farm. It holds a turned oak dibber for pricking out, plastic labels and marker pens, a ball of green twine on a holder so that it doesn't get tangled and plastic-coated wire. There are various sets of gloves from the builders merchants, and an oiled tarp with handles. This is brilliant. I throw it over the garden table when potting out, gather piles of leaves onto it in the autumn, and cover plants when I am moving them so that they don't dry out. Then there's the fleece, on a roll so that it is always to hand. I don't know what we did before fleece and it is incredibly useful here, keeping the cats, birds and, to a degree, the foxes off the young plants.

My cloches are on their last legs and, one day, when I am flush and they have finally given up, I will replace them with glass. For now, the corrugated plastic is perfect, giving a good two months' protection early in the season. They are also easily dismantled and stored in the garage. The cold frame is another life-saver, and the two square metres of protected space that it provides has allowed me to start propagating again. It is never empty, with bulbs and overwintering cuttings in winter, tender annuals that are in transition in spring, and basil, cuttings and young seedlings in the growing season.

PAGE 51
Frost damage.

Winter

Beauty in the Wreckage

Sometime late in November the frost sneaks into the lower parts of the garden. It is surreptitious at first and goes largely unnoticed but, before the year is out, the freeze will have made its presence felt. The nasturtiums are the litmus test and the first to show frost damage. They are often at their best at this point, having run amok once I let the garden go in the autumn. Their foliage charts the progress of the freeze as it works towards the shelter of the house until one day I find their remains draped limp and lifeless up by the terrace like bedraggled party streamers.

The garden goes into a marvellous decline from this point onwards – a decline that day by day sees the greens replaced by browns, and a new transparency return to the skyline. Fences, boundaries and neighbouring houses come back into focus and a new lightness makes its way into the beds as the foliage falls away. The mood is not one of sadness, for it is a relief that the garden is relaxing into itself. I feel let off the hook to a degree, and gardening is confined to little more than sweeping the terraces to create a line of demarcation between the tended areas and those being left to go through the natural cycle.

Imposing a little order goes a long way at this time of the year, but I leave the vegetation in the beds because there is beauty in the wreckage. While only some of the plants in the garden die with dignity, those that do have currency, and they hold the garden together over the coming months with their sculptural remains. Their skeletons halt the winter light when it slides in at a tilt and provide us with form and

Decaying foliage of *Hydrangea aspera* Villosa Group.

PAGE 56
Skeletons of *Clematis heracleifolia* 'Cassandra' and *Cleome hassleriana* (syn. *spinosa*).

structure and the memory of the season past. Some days the garden is a flurry of tits feeding on verbena seed, and blackbirds scraping the leaf litter to locate any worms that have come up to the surface. The darkened remains of the *Eryngium*, the silvery *Panicum* and the *Cephalaria dipsacoides* are also a winter home to the insects that live here, too. Their hollow stems provide hibernacula for the ladybirds, and an accumulation of mulch protects the slug-eating ground beetles.

One of the primary reasons for leaving the garden be at this point is for the natural cycle to remain uninterrupted. Decay hits fast and in no time the plants that do not have the stamina to stand as skeletons are reduced to nothing. The worms play a big part in this, pulling the rotting foliage back into their burrows where it is recycled into humus. This is an all-important part of keeping the soil in good condition, for the leaf litter feeds the worms, and the worms keep the soil free-draining and hearty.

The garden changes daily in its slow, sure reduction, and I wish that certain plants had more endurance, for it would be nice to depend upon them for longer. Where many ornamental grasses such as *Miscanthus* and *Calamagrostis* endure until the spring, the *Molinia caerulea* subsp. *arundinacea* has fallen by the beginning of January. The editing process happens only where it is needed and I remove those plants that no longer offer aesthetic value or complicate the upstanding skeletons around them. Although the great clear-up won't happen until the bulbs are coming through at the end of February, the compost heap recycles what has not already been drawn into the earth by the worms and their allies.

Miscanthus nepalensis.

Leaving the skeletons also means that certain plants have a chance at seeding. Of those that you want to seed, like the poppies (opium and Welsh) and the *Tulipa sprengeri* with its rattle-shaped seed heads, this is a bonus, but certain plants risk becoming an issue over time. The *Allium hollandicum* 'Purple Sensation' is a prolific seeder and, as they get away early in spring and their growth is lush, they smother anything that is slow to get off the blocks. In just three years, the rash of youngsters threatens to overwhelm smaller plants such as the neighbouring *Iris chrysographes* and *Gillennia trifoliata*, and I have now started to remove their seed heads before they ripen completely. A degree of control at the right time is all that is needed to strike the balance and save time weeding in the spring.

Cannas are perfectly hardy in London, but I like to leave the leaf for the cover it affords the rhizomes in the tougher winters. The leaves are also rather extraordinary in their death throes, like curing leather hanging out to dry or foliage cast in bronze. However, there comes a time when you have to make way for the future and this is usually triggered by the bulbs, which are woven through the perennials. This is all part of working with the cycle, not pushing against it by slashing and burning to get the garden shipshape for the winter. By the time new life is pushing through to replace the old, I am done with the skeletons and happy to move on.

Right Plant, Right Place

Few things are more pleasurable than planting. Through the action of setting something new into well-prepared ground, you are not only realizing plans, which are sometimes long-invested, but also engaging in the future. As you push the soil around the roots and stand back to admire, you see not the twig or the tiny nub of growth now almost covered by the mulch around it, but a future lived out in growth.

Although I must admit to getting better at it, a good number of the plants in my garden have been moved at least once to find the optimum position. A planting is like a jigsaw puzzle – every piece is interdependent and you have to know your medium to judge how each will influence its neighbours. It takes time to understand a plant's nature – a minimum of five years with a perennial and considerably longer with anything woody – so a practical starting point is key to good judgment. The first consideration (or at least one that has to be made in tandem with aesthetics) is whether you are choosing 'the right plant for the right place'. This Beth Chatto mantra makes perfect sense. Why attempt to force a plant to do what you want it to when it has evolved over millennia to fit into a specific ecological niche? Of course, many plants are adaptable, which is why we are able to combine plants from many different parts of the world, but having their native habitat in mind is always the best starting point.

I learned this lesson early as a child, when I pined for sun and a hearty soil capable of supporting moisture-lovers, although we were gardening on thin, acidic sand in woodland. The plants that did well there thrived in the dappled shade and I was taunted by the conditions at the garden that I went to on a Saturdays to earn my pocket money. The late Mrs Frances Pumphrey, a great gardener of local fame, owned Greatham Mill. Set in a small Hampshire valley, with a stream at the bottom which fed the Mill, Mrs P. had started to garden around the house forty years before. She was an exuberant gardener and her husband, The Captain, who farmed the valley, had had to erect a fence to stop her going any further. By the time I arrived, there were several

acres of ornamental planting and a wealth of different habitats.
I soaked up her acquired knowledge and experience like a sponge.
At the end of a day's work, I would cycle up the hill, my panniers
weighed down by gifts and plants that I had bought in her nursery.

Mrs P. had spent years experimenting and the plants always came
with good advice. In spite of this, I learned the hard way that the
candelabra primulas, which thrived on her moisture-retentive clay,
dwindled to nothing on our sandy soil unless they were constantly
watered. My *Gunnera* struggled in a depression I had lined with
polythene and continued to do so until I moved it to the damp ground
by the overflow from the cesspit. The silver-leaved and Mediterranean
plants loved the free-draining ground but, in the shady woodland, they
strained towards the light. I continued to fail until I gradually learned
from experience that you had to work with the nature of a plant and not
against it just because you wanted it. I also learned that for every failure
there was a plant that would like you once you had pinpointed its
weaknesses and strengths. The learning curve still continues and it has
been a big part of this garden as I use it to refine and add to my palette.

After looking at the specifics of what likes to grow where, the next
most important consideration is what it will grow with. If you can
combine things that favour the same conditions, you can start to build
up communities of balanced partnerships. One will fend for the other
by perhaps offering it shade or shelter from wind. The *Epimedium
wushanense* is a good example of a plant that needs to be grown in
combination, for out in the open the delicate leaves are damaged by
spring winds. They grow here in the shelter of the box and the
bamboo. The air is damp and still, which is perfect for the *Rodgersia*
and the ferns that favour the same conditions. As a group, the
provenance of the plants is diverse, but their demands are similar and
their habits complementary.

Planting

I have always enjoyed planting properly and believe in the old adage,
'Spend a penny on the plant and a pound on the hole'. It is a practice
I follow strictly here, which is why the compost heap retains such
importance. The garden has changed extensively since the first round
of planting and, whenever I replant an area, I always enrich the soil
with the addition of compost or manure. This is necessary on most
soils, whether they need it to retain moisture or to open up the
structure to allow free movement of air and water.

Although manure and compost don't contain masses of nutrients, they do provide a better environment for the bacteria that help to liberate minerals. Minerals are supplemented in the form of slow-release organic fertilizers, such as blood, fish and bone. Bonemeal and granulated seaweed are equally good, and I keep a stockpile in the garage so that they are always to hand. Unlike the fast food provided by inorganic fertilizers, the minerals from the slow-release organics are liberated only when the ground temperature is warm enough for the bacteria to be active. This is also when the plants are in active growth and require sustenance.

The season for planting bare-root plants is any time between the end of September and the end of March. The earlier you can get them in the ground during that period, the better, as the hair roots will make connection with their new environment in all but the most frozen conditions. Here, in London, this means we can plant almost anytime the soil is not completely saturated. A plant that has had the chance to get its roots in contact with the soil before top growth starts in earnest will have access to water and minerals and is in a stronger position come the growing season. The later you leave it, the more you will have to cosset and water when the plant comes into growth.

Pot-grown plants can be put in at any time of the year, as long as the soil is not frozen or waterlogged but, if the compost is dry, it is always worth plunging the pots in a bucket of water until bubbles stop coming to the surface. I like to water in after planting to settle the soil around the roots, and it is worth remembering that newly planted evergreens also need water in their first winter, as the leaves are continuing to transpire. I learned this lesson the hard way after planting the bamboos here in the autumn. Although I had dug in heaps of compost to give them a good start and soaked the root balls before planting, the roots had not had the time to make proper contact with the ground before the tops were blasted by drying winter winds. All eight plants defoliated in a week in their first February and I panicked for two months until they finally pushed out replacement leaves. The bamboos had, in fact, been protecting their reserves of moisture by shedding their foliage, but had made me feel very uncomfortable in the process.

I am somewhat obsessive about giving my plants a good start in life and will ponder each and every corner to match the plant to the environment that is on offer. Over time, the microclimate in the garden has changed as things have grown up and provided me with shelter, and I have had to adapt as the shelter has increased. The prairie plants and steppe-land grasses that favoured the conditions here when things were more open have been mostly ousted and now I prize the sunny corners where once I prized the shade. Though I want and aim to get things right, I experiment here, too, as this is my garden and I can afford to make mistakes so I will push the boundaries. Will the soil be friable and free-draining enough now that I have improved it to keep the *Arisaema* from damping off in the winter, and will the *Nicotiana mutabilis* be perennial if they are given the shelter up by the fence? You cannot afford to do this with clients but the garden here is a laboratory and it allows me to make better informed judgments in the future.

I make sure that a planting hole is at least a third bigger than the root ball or container. The soil around the roots should be friable and easy for roots to venture into but not overly enriched with compost because this will simply provide a safe place from which the roots will venture no further. Again, it is all about balance, and I mulch new plantings to conserve moisture and suppress competition. It is also an easy way of working goodness into the soil since the earthworms do the work for you.

Staking is minimal here, as I like things to stand on their own, but young trees are usually given something to help them gain a foothold. I short-stake, using a support no more than a third of the height of the trunk to allow it to flex and build up strength where it bends in the wind. You do not want your plants to become reliant upon stakes, and some mobility helps to promote root growth in all directions. A stake should not be needed after the second growing season but now that I have the shelter, I can reduce that to a year.

Evergreen

Even though autumn is over, the *Cercis* often hangs onto a solitary crimson leaf until Christmas. You can see through its cage of growth again and, as the garden beyond retreats into itself, it appears to shrink in scale. With the cloak of vegetation cast to the ground, you can once again see the structure of things, and your eye begins to travel to the boundaries. Our neighbours at the end are visible once more and, as the winter progresses and frost takes out the last of the perennials, I become patently aware of my rectangle of ground prescribed by walls and fences.

When we moved here in November 1997, it was impossible to tell where one thing began and the other ended because the thicket of brambles occupying the middle third of the garden was busily jumping the fences. Despite the air of neglect, it was a lesson in never revealing everything at once, and the clearing beyond the thicket was

The last leaf on the *Cercis canadensis* 'Forest Pansy'.

a surprise, or a gift. The leaves had already fallen from the dilapidated fruit trees, but the evergreen of the briars created the illusion that the garden ran further than it did. When the brambles were grubbed out later that winter, I was shocked and shocked again at the starkness of the plot, but I held onto the memory of what they did in terms of fooling the imagination.

A garden revealed all at once is like a story told before it is started. Evergreens play an important part in holding something back, not only in what lies beyond them, but also in what the garden becomes when it settles into its wintry state. The winter garden needs bone structure, while the summer garden also depends upon their gravity as a foil. The Victorians gave evergreens their bad reputation, planting them profusely and at the expense of more ephemeral plants. The constancy and weight of aucuba, yew, box, privet and holly took a heavy toll because there was no relief from the wall of green. You need to have evergreen in conjunction with the deciduous to allow the seasons in.

Box forms and fallen *Molinia*.

To avoid them becoming the dominating force, evergreens should be used with levity. Light should be allowed to fall to earth in the winter and, with it, room given for deciduous plants to come and go among them in summer. The garden here would feel empty without the evergreens, but they probably take up no more than a fifth of the ground. Looking out there now, on a still December day, the garden is far from naked and the evergreens conceal and reveal like the wings of a set in a theatre. If I had a larger space in which to indulge formality, I would create structure with evergreens providing the line, but here, where informality rules, the weight of greenery is soft and informal, except for the clipped mound of the box by the decking.

I like the box for its constancy and calm, and the mound creates the 'waist', or a restricted pinch point, before the open clearing at the end. Part of it started life on my roof garden in Vauxhall as a topiary bird, which I beheaded when it arrived here because the body made the perfect shape for the prow of the mound. The box is cut after the extension growth has ripened in June and this is enough to keep it trim for the remainder of the year. I have been lucky with box blight so far, which has not found its way into the garden, and I keep the plants clean and airy at ground level by carefully removing the box clippings. Although the browning that occurs from time to time has fooled me into thinking they have blight, I have been relieved to discover it is the tomcats in the neighbourhood using them as a marker post. No matter – the box grows out of the damage, and growth around it is dense enough to inhibit the toms for most of the summer.

The garden tends to look smaller in the winter, when the evergreens become most apparent, so I work with smaller foliage, which doesn't act as a focal point. The winter box *Sarcococca ruscifolia* at the front and the myrtle *Myrtus communis* against the hot fence are also kept trimmed. Small leaves help with that, too, as the cuts are rarely evident on a leaf that is small and merges into the mass. Both make good hedging; the winter box in the cool, the myrtle in the heat and sunshine. The *Sarcococca hookeriana* var. *dignya* is not for clipping, as its arching growth and larger leaf would not respond favourably. I have the form called 'Purple Stem' with long, chocolate-green leaves.

Although they have considerably more presence, the *Phyllostachys* are also chosen for the slightness of the leaf. Not all bamboos have small foliage, and those with larger leaves are more demanding as a result. There are two *Phyllostachys* here: *P. viridiglaucescens* to conceal the pink brick wall of the garages at the end, and *P. nigra* to give privacy to the terrace. The seasons have little effect on this barrier, and the terrace remains private all year with this screen in place.

The green of the evergreens is also something to consider. The brilliant emerald of the *Euphorbia mellifera* is uplifting and it has proven to be lush and happy on the north side of the fence. It livens up the shade here, and the dark winter foliage of *Epimedium* x *perralchicum* 'Fröhnleiten' at its feet further heightens the luminosity of the lime in the leaf. If I had the room, I would have holly for its darkness in winter. As long as it is placed so that the sun can fall upon it, it is never oppressive because the leaves are reflective and shine like a thousand tiny mirrors. Though not as dark, as a winter backdrop the lustrous leaves of the *Rosa* 'Cooperi' and the dark, simple leaf of the ivy *Hedera colchica* at the end of the garden work in much the same way. I am careful not to line the boundaries with plants that simply re-establish the enclosure when the rest of the leaves are down. The weight of foliage is juggled so that it never lies heavy, with breathing space between the evergreens so that the seasons can come and go among them.

Euphorbia mellifera.

Front Garden

When we arrived here, a severed ivy, browned and clinging on regardless, festooned the stucco at the front of the house like a filthy beard. Sooty mould smothered the masonry, the path and the struggling *Senecio*. The reason for the mould was the lime tree planted by the railings, and a million aphids rained a slick of honeydew from the branches when the tree was in leaf. The lime had heaved the wall

PAGE 65
Daphne bholua 'Jacqueline Postill'.

PAGES 66–7
Crocosmia 'Lucifer'.

PAGES 68–9
A posy of *Hamamelis* x *intermedia* 'Jelena', *Arum italicum* subsp. *italicum* 'Marmoratum', *Clematis cirrhosa* var. *purpurascens* 'Freckles' and *Sarcococca ruscifolia* var. *chinensis* 'Dragon Gate'.

PAGES 70–1
The 'hot' border under snow.

and with it the railings and, despite an obvious reduction some time in the past, its highest limbs brushed the roof slates fifteen metres above the ground. The squirrels used them as a highway to their quarters in the loft.

I was not a fan of the lime and I had it reduced by a third in the first winter in preparation for its eventual removal. This took place over two years, with a second third removed the following winter before the final felling in the spring of the third year. This slow process was to allow the ground under the tree to rehydrate slowly and avoid the possibility of heave. It was a relief when it was finally dissected and taken down. It was too big for its position and had suffered over the years as a result of various attempts to keep it within bounds.

By the time it came down, I had cleared the front garden and laid a York stone path across the bed to connect the front steps with the parking space to the side. In the process, I unearthed a colony of *Cyclamen hederifolium*, but the soil was poor and impoverished. On reflection, I now wish that I had bitten the bullet and replaced the soil. The stump of the lime was left in the ground, even though it could have encouraged honey fungus, but I took the risk because we had already seen stag beetles in the garden and I knew that rotting stumps were home to their larvae. Ever since, on the first warm nights in early June, the beetles have appeared and, to date, the honey fungus has claimed no more victims.

We are lucky to have a very proactive tree officer in the Borough of Southwark and, in conjunction with getting permission to remove the lime, I had negotiated its replacement with a street tree. I was sent the council's approved tree list and decided on a young *Liquidambar styraciflua*. Although I did no more than water it well for the first three years, it has outstripped the other young trees planted in the same winter that have had to get by on council water rations. Ten years later, it now fills the second- and third-floor windows with a fiery glow when it colours in the autumn and helps to contribute to the feeling of privacy and the illusion that the garden runs beyond our boundaries.

Despite measuring no more than three metres in depth, the front garden is essential to our privacy, as it provides a buffer from the pavement; a place between home and the city beyond. The house faces east, and the garden here has already seen several different planting schemes come and go in an effort to find what suits the space. After the lime came down, we felt exposed enough to plant a bamboo hedge, which stopped the eyes of passers-by from looking through our windows. But the Oriental mood of bamboo rarely looks right at the front of a Victorian house and it was soon moved to where it sits more

Cyclamen hederifolium.

PAGE 72
Helleborus x *ericsmithii* and *Arum italicum* subsp. *italicum* 'Marmoratum'.

comfortably at the back. It was replaced with two *Genista aetnensis* that I had initially tried in the back garden. These Mediterranean trees have thrived in the thin, free-draining soil and a position that loses the sun by midday. Their net of branches acts as a veil, and their rapid growth has covered for the slower growth of the *Liquidambar*.

The *Genista* show little change throughout the year since the leaves are no more than scales. However, when in bloom, they mark the season in spectacular fashion. Some time in early June, tiny pea flowers begin their accumulation and, for two weeks to either side of the longest day, the trees hang heavy and heady with the honey-scented blossom. When they are in flower, the light in the front rooms turns golden but, after ten years, I am now faced with the dilemma of whether to remove one or both to allow the *Liquidambar* more room. Though poor, the soil is not as poor as it would be on the slopes of Mount Etna, where the tree broom has its home, and they have grown too rapidly at the expense of stability. The one resting at a jaunty angle on the brick pier to the railings will most probably be the first to go. It is worth noting that, in just a decade, the incarnation of a garden can already have gone through its first cycle.

Iris unguicularis 'Mary Barnard'.

The Banksian rose over the porch is also yellow. I have chosen yellows here, as they make you feel that the sun is out even though it leaves the front of the house by lunchtime. The yellows are balanced with plenty of green and white. *Hydrangea quercifolia* 'Snow Queen' is chosen as much for its evergreen oak-shaped foliage as the flower. This hydrangea needs sun to flower well, as does the white-flowered *Crinum* x *powellii*, and they get just enough for both to make an effort. The hydrangea is sheltered here and keeps its foliage through the winter when it would lose it in a colder position.

The actual area of planting in the front garden is modest, but I have aimed for there to be something of interest throughout the year, as the kitchen window in the half-basement looks directly onto this space. A unifying cover of *Viola labradorica* (*V. riviniana* Purpurea Group) helps to make up for the poor soil and the dry conditions created by the rain shadow of the house. Through it emerges a series of seasonal events up close to the window: the snowdrop *Galanthus* 'S. Arnott', *Helleborus* x *ericsmithii* and *Iris unguicularis* 'Mary Barnard' in winter; *Epimedium davidii* and *Ranunculus ficaria* 'Jake Perry' in spring; *Geranium macrorrhizum* 'White-Ness' (better than the off-white of the form known as 'Album') and the painted fern in summer prolong interest and there is rarely a downtime here. I have added to the pink *Cyclamen hederifolium* with the white form and a silver-leaved selection. They perform for months, first with autumnal flower and then winter foliage. The flowers are joined in October with the marbled foliage of *Arum italicum* subsp. *italicum* 'Marmoratum', which I love for its out-of-season freshness.

Winter is an important season at the front of the house since we spend a lot of time inside looking through the window. *Helleborus* x *ericsmithii* and *Iris unguicularis* 'Mary Barnard' are given the warmest positions, as they need all the light they can get. Both like the free-draining soil and seem perfectly happy with poor ground after being given a good start. The *Acanthus mollis* 'Hollard's Gold' are also at their best in the winter months, with foliage that is lush and rude with health. I first came to understand the seasonal habits of *Acanthus* when I saw them growing among the Corinthian columns strewn by the roadside in Rome. It was February and they had responded to the winter rains by making bulk of their growth. Revisit them in the drought of the summer and the only clues that they have been there are the mildewed remains of the flower spikes. In London, where it is mild enough for them to keep their foliage, they do much the same. They have a downtime after flowering when the mildew strikes, but cut them to the base in August and water heavily and the foliage is back by October. They do take a couple of years to settle into this routine, as their roots are deep and moisture-searching. Top growth is minimal until they have their footing, but they live for decades without division. A little shade helps to keep 'Hollard's Gold' on the emerald side of gold, which tempers things a little.

Evergreens provide a backdrop to the seasonal comings and goings, and the *Clematis cirrhosa* var. *purpurascens* 'Freckles' has taken over the railings and has to be prevented from travelling up into the *Genista*, where it gains purchase on low branches. It needs a warm position to do well, but it obviously likes life here and looks after itself without any more demands. From November through to February, it is hung with creamy bells, which, if you turn them up and look inside, are speckled with maroon. This 'hedge' of clematis is all we need to make the division between the common ground of the pavement and our ground, and it does so handsomely.

Acanthus mollis 'Hollard's Gold'.

Clematis cirrhosa var. *purpurascens* 'Freckles'.

Scent

Scent is key in teasing the senses. It catches you when you are least prepared for stimulus and takes you somewhere unexpected. I like to play with perfume throughout the year, and throughout the garden, and it is particularly important in the planting at the front of the house, as it introduces you to the garden while you are still on the pavement. First impressions set the tone, and the perfume here is mollifying and intriguing. Where you have been closed to the sensory overload of the city, it opens you up without obviously demanding anything and by the time you get to the front door, you have already begun your journey.

Although it is easier to reap the benefits of perfume on the still, warm air of summer, it is the winter-scented plants that are most memorable. They stand out at a time of year when all of the senses are under wraps. Three winter box (*Sarcococca*) are planted together to create a unified group and between them they perfume the whole of the front garden. They are a form of *Sarcococca ruscifolia* var. *chinensis* called 'Dragon Gate' and they sit well in the small space here because their foliage is finer and their growth more graceful than the parent. Although they have been slow to attain a presence, I can see that they will be easy to keep in check, and they respond well to pruning after they have flowered. The buds are already visible in November and, by the beginning of December, the very first are open. They are extremely small, not much more than tufts among the foliage and, initially, you have to stoop to get the benefit of the scent. By Christmas, there are enough to create quite a cloud of sweetness, and more will come throughout the month of January. Small sprigs, complete with red berries, are picked for the house. They don't last much more than a day inside, but a tiny branch will scent a room, and the cuttings can be kept for rooting if they are put in a pot of free-draining compost. Accompanying them early in the year are the large flowers of the hybrid snowdrop *Galanthus* 'S. Arnott'. This is also perfumed if you bring a flower to your nose, a sweet primrosey smell on cold air.

As the winter box wanes in February, the first buds on the *Daphne bholua* 'Jacqueline Postill' begin to break. I imagine *D. bholua* straggling through open woodland in its native habitat in the Himalayas and feel for it here, sandwiched between my boundary wall and the car. In the five years that it has been here, it is already taller than I am and, though I have the feeling that it has reached its ultimate height and will soon begin to spread, its upright habit is fine in this position. The semi-evergreen foliage, which thins as the flowers drain the plant's energy, is enough to screen me from my neighbours, who benefit from the scent more than I do, as the prevailing wind moves down the street. In fact, on still, damp days, you can smell the daphne at the end of the street as you approach the house, and the perfume loiters heavily in the front garden. The flowers of 'Jacqueline Postill' are from another era, a sugary mauvish-pink, like the old-fashioned rose Cachous, and the scent is as sweet and talcy as your grandmother's dressing room.

Sarcococca ruscifolia var. *chinensis* 'Dragon Gate'.

Daphne bholua 'Darjeeling'.

I have secreted two more forms in shady places in the garden to get to know them. 'Darjeeling' is the palest pink, fading to white, and flowers first at the end of December, while the more tightly growing 'Alba' has a smaller flower that is pure white. Between the three of them, I have flowers and scent from December until the end of March.

The *Holboellia latifolia* on the cool fence always catches me out in April with its tropical lily-of-the-valley scent. The event lasts a week, maybe two, with the curious greenish-pink flowers hanging in clusters under the leaves. I have used this evergreen climber to balance the *Trachelospermum jasminoides* on the sunny side of the garden. It seems happy in a little shade, whereas the evergreen jasmine prefer the light, and between them they weave an exotic overlay into the planting. The *Trachelospermum* even covers for the stench of the carrion-scented *Dracunculus vulgaris* when it flowers in June and, of all the climbers, it serves me best by perfuming the garden for weeks on end in the high summer months.

I would find it hard to garden without the summer-flowering magnolias, and love the simple, primitive beauty of their flowers. Not all have liked me – *Magnolia sieboldii* subsp. *sinensis* hated living here and scorched, despite being cosseted and given a shaded position. I replaced it with *M.* x *wieseneri* 'Aashild Kalleberg', which has a similar flower but upturned where the *M. sinensis* is pendulous. I mourn the loss but, if something fails, it is always worth trying a relative. *Magnolia* 'Porcelain Dove' is looking like it will be better suited here and will enjoy the warmth as many of the magnolias do. It has large, pale green foliage, which is silvered on the undersides. A succession of creamy flowers opens over six weeks from early May, one or two at a time, and you want to bury yourself in the flower. It smells heavy and zesty all at once, of churches, incense and musk, and the zest of limes and lemons.

The pots help me work in perfume where it is lacking and where it is needed. A small pot of *Dianthus*, smelling of cloves, and night-scented *Nicotiana suaveolens* or *Lilium regale* can be brought up close to the house or moved to pivotal passing places. Knowing how the air moves through your garden is an important part of placing scented plants and you should aim to harness the breeze so that it moves towards you and away from the plant. Better still is to hold the perfume within an enclosure. Pacing the perfume is also something that I consider carefully – the lilies come in succession so that *Lilium regale* 'African Queen' and Golden Splendor Group pick up where *Lilium regale* leaves off in early July.

Night-scented plants create a particular magic. *Gladiolus tristis* has the palest chartreuse wands of flower, which start the season early in May. It is a surprising plant, packing a perfume like cloves that's not dissimilar to stocks, but it needs an open position to do its best. I bought my bulbs from Great Dixter in East Sussex, where it is planted in the heat of the sunken garden. I only discovered the nocturnal perfume some years later when I lived with it myself and experienced it after sundown. *Hemerocallis altissima* is, as the name suggests, the tallest day lily. The flowers open at dusk and are also sweetly scented. The *Brugmansia arborea* is almost certainly the most highly scented plant in the garden. It literally 'switches on' at about six o'clock in the evening. The lush, heady scent gives away something of the narcotic nature of this plant and even though the perfume itself isn't hallucinogenic, you feel as if it might be and automatically keep your distance. I have three growing in the garden now, although they have to be hauled back to the garage in winter for protection. On a still summer evening, you can feel the weight of the perfume as it fingers its way through the garden and lies waiting for you in the hollows. It is somewhere between vanilla and musk with citrus overtones, and is sweet, zesty and dirty all in the same breath. It could not be more exotic and it transports you somewhere else entirely when it catches you unawares.

Hamamelis

An old friend of mine who worked at the Kalmthout Arboretum in Belgium once took me to meet the real-life Jelena many years before I grew to love the witch hazel named after her. It was late summer and Mrs Jelena de Belder, whose husband Robert had bred the plant, was up a ladder at the front of the house picking grapes for teatime. She sent me up there to finish the job before we had our tea and were shown around the garden. I did not know then, because it wasn't their season, that I would fall for the witch hazels quite so keenly, nor that so many of the hybrids that I have learned to depend upon were the life-work of this husband-and-wife team.

Now that I have taken the time to grow *Hamamelis* x *intermedia* 'Jelena', it is nice to think that Mr de Belder knew a good thing when he saw it. I bought a young plant not long after moving here and put it in a pot so that it could be brought up close to the house in the dark months. Space here for shrubs is limited and I needed to get to know it before finding it a permanent home. I quickly found that, as long as *Hamamelis* are given a little summer shade and never allowed to dry out in the growing season, they are more than happy containerized. Very soon I had quite a collection.

There is not a chance that 'Jelena' will make it up to the terrace now because it has been repotted several times over the last decade and is now too unwieldy to bump down the steps. I can still drag the pot across the deck from where it is kept in the cooling influence of the hornbeam, and I do this as soon as the first flowers pop so that they flare in the low winter sunshine that grazes the fence. Some plants need light in the flowers and *Hamamelis* is one. Each twist of petal, like dried orange zest, seems to catch its own ray of light and, when the horizontal branches are illuminated, it is the only plant in the garden you can look at.

Hamamelis x *intermedia* 'Gingerbread'.

On occasional years, 'Jelena' has kept its foliage into the winter, which is a trait of several of the *Hamamelis* x *intermedia* hybrids when they are young, but most years the leaves drop as normal. They colour well before they do, in shades of orange, saffron and apricot. Not long after leaf drop, you soon become aware of the clusters of buds. They are super matte and a velvety cinnamon-brown. 'Jelena' is well known for being one of the earliest to flower and, in a warm winter, the first buds have broken by Christmas, but late January or early February is the more usual time. You are ready for life by this point in the winter and, without fail, I never tire of the month or five weeks when the witch hazels are out. One crinkled petal will usually unroll itself ahead of the rest to alert you but, within days, the flowers are festooning the branches. Each filament has a dark maroon base, with the colour fading to a warm burnt orange. The petals are crumpled, like unfurled crushed tissue paper and, amid the flowers, there are usually a few woody seed cases from the previous season.

Hamamelis x *intermedia* 'Barmstedt Gold'.

Once established, *Hamamelis* are happy in an open position, but by choice they prefer to occupy similar conditions to the European hazel. They like a glade or the edge of woodland with cool air and summer moisture at their feet. Although they favour acid conditions or soil that is neutral, I have grown them in alkaline ground where the soil is deep and moisture-retentive, with added organic matter.

I can forgive 'Jelena' for having just the smallest hint of orange zest perfume and I have made up for it with other varieties here. 'Barmstedt Gold' (one of the best *H.* x *intermedia* yellows) is independently luminous, as the flowers have the colour of the sun in them already. The rusty 'Gingerbread', which is zesty and sharp on cold air, has the added benefit of chocolate-tinted young foliage. I also have a plant of *Hamamelis mollis*, which is better scented than them all. I have tried several reds here over the years, namely *H.* x *intermedia* 'Rubin', 'Livia' and 'Diane', but their comparative darkness needs careful placing so that the sun can illuminate them.

One day, when I have land enough to be able to plant a glade in which they can glow in winter, I will plant the best of those that have been passing through the garden as pot plants. They usually stay for five or six years until they are too big to cluster together in the shade of the hornbeam and then they are given a home with clients or friends, where I can watch them to check on progress, as you might with godchildren living at a distance.

Winter Pruning

The process of pruning should be like a conversation, allowing you to identify a plant's strengths and weaknesses and ensure its well-being and garden-worthiness. It is your opportunity to plot the future into the framework and overcome a chequered past, storm damage, leaning and breakages. Standing back and taking stock before the interaction should be part of the process and this is never better done than in the nakedness of winter. A well-trained tree or shrub, helped to attain perfection by pruning rather than being butchered into submission, is a pleasure if you can see the care in the branches. There has to be a reason to prune, and I do so to keep a plant within bounds, to encourage a good outline or to contain it within a position. I also prune for good health, for vigour, for fruit and for flower.

Life starts early along the south-facing fence and, even at its lowest, the sun never fails to dip into the garden. The *Clematis* x *triternata* 'Rubromarginata' is usually the first indication that the sap is rising and I have to remember to look under the nest of last year's growth to check that the new shoots haven't got away without me noticing. This and the small-flowered, summer-flowering *Clematis viticella* are resistant to the clematis wilt I have struggled with here, and they could not be easier to look after, as long as you put in the time early in the season to tie in the soft new shoots. These are alarmingly brittle if they start to grow in the wrong direction, so fanning them out while they are new is the best way to ensure good coverage later.

Pruning the summer-flowering clematis is straightforward, but the reason you want to do this no later than the end of February is to save the energy in the base of the plant. If you leave it much later, the sap will be wasted in shoots forming higher up on last year's growth. This produces an unruly plant with smaller flowers over a shorter season, leaving bare ankles in its wake. In a garden this size, where the fences are not the best feature, it is good to keep the plants clothed to the base.

Felco No. 2 secateurs.

PAGE 81
Ranunculus ficaria 'Brazen Hussy'.

PAGES 82–3
Hamamelis x *intermedia* 'Rubin'.

PAGES 84–5
The end of winter clear-up.

PAGES 86–7
Galanthus nivalis and Green Spotted form of *Helleborus orientalis*.

I prune clematis to about knee height, to a framework of the strongest stems. A clean cut, just above a bud, is all that is required to focus the plant into new, manageable growth, and the remains of last year are taken to the compost heap. This early growth is the reminder that the sap is stirring elsewhere and, before the end of February, I make sure that the grapevines are reduced back to their framework. Vines bleed if you prune them too late and, though I have risked doing so out of necessity in the past, I like to work to their natural dormancy and keep the goodness in the plant instead of causing it to weep away from a tardy cut.

I prune both the vines to the same set of rules but to achieve different results. The strawberry grape, *Vitis vinifera* 'Fragola', is a variety that I grow for a sense of well-being as much as anything. It has a pretty, simple leaf that rarely succumbs to mildew and, given a sunny aspect, it is a reliable cropper. The fruits have a curious taste, though, somewhere between an artificial strawberry flavour and bubble gum, but I like the feeling of abundance that they bring to the end of the garden. I grow the crimson glory vine, *V. coignetiae*, on a north-facing wall because the shade there enhances the size of the leaf. Pruning hard puts all the energy into the leaves, which magnifies their size even more.

There are few things more satisfying than setting a plant up properly from the beginning so that it clothes what you want it to and looks the part in the winter. In the first three years, the vines are trained into an evenly spaced framework of primary limbs and, once the skeleton is in place, it is simply a case of reducing last year's growth back hard to one or two buds. This encourages a fruiting spur, which goes on to produce the grapes on the 'Fragola'.

The wisteria on the west-facing back of the house was the first plant I put in the garden twelve years ago and I have deliberately trained it slowly rather than letting it rush towards the light. You can see the organization in the limbs and the decisions I have made to make it flower well for me. A limb trained horizontally will be much more inclined to produce spurring branches, and flowers, than one left to ascend. Ascending is their nature, and a branch trained sideways in the summer will quickly stop at the growing tip and 'break' where it has been bent over. My method, while establishing the rangy framework, is to take advantage of this upward habit and allow new limbs to ascend in the summer. They are taken off the wires in the winter and carefully trained sideways so that in the growing season they break along their length to form laterals that can then be encouraged to form flowering spurs.

PAGE 88
A selection of *Helleborus* x *hybridus*, best floated in water when cut.

Now that I have the framework that I need, I follow the standard method of reducing all summer growth to eight buds in August. This encourages the wood to ripen and spurs to form close to the original framework. In the winter, these same shoots are cut back to two buds and, over the years, the flowering branches grow to form a woody 'antler'. The advantage of the antlers is that they are held away from the wall, which, in the *Wisteria floribunda* 'Alba' that I have here, allows the pendulous racemes to hang freely in space.

Unless a plant is sickly or weak, pruning nearly always promotes the response of growth, so an essential part of every pruning exercise is to follow through with a feeding regime. A handful of blood, fish and bone, spread evenly every square metre in the root zone, equips your plants for the summer ahead. If you have it to hand, a mulch of compost or well-rotted manure will help preserve moisture so that growth can easily be replenished.

Clear-Up

New life is making its way through the dwindling skeletons and there comes a point towards the end of February when the garden begins to look the worse for wear. The bulbs are the prompt that it is time to make a start on the great clear-up and, when the balance tips, it is hard not to want the garden shipshape. I avoid the temptation to wade in and make a clean sweep, and pace myself to draw the process out. It is a time to be thorough, a time to set things up for the year ahead, and a mistake to clear too quickly, as the garden will look naked and raw, like a room stripped of furniture and waiting to be occupied.

That said, the bulbs are fast to get away when the weather is mild, and I clear where I am mulching before the bulbs spear the ground to avoid the fiddle of working between the emerging growth. It makes sense to liberate these areas first. The *Persicaria* under the hydrangea is cleared in January to make way for the snowdrops. The foliage of the *Nectaroscordum* is also early to rise, and the celandines strain under the debris of last year's perennials if left too long into February.

I make a start by preparing the compost heaps. The empty bin will be home to this season's debris, so I bed it down with the loose topping from the heap beside it. The crust of the current heap soon gives way to compost, but the roughest, partially decomposed compost near the top is thrown into the awaiting bin. The worms and the bacteria in this layer act as a 'starter' for the new heap and, with the old heap now ready to use, I can mulch as I go when clearing.

There are few things more satisfying than pulling the wreckage of the winter away to reveal new growth. Though it will be a while yet before shoots on most of the perennials start to swell and break away from their crowns, they are clearly there and ready for the off. Pull the spent foliage of the peony Molly-the-witch (*Paeonia mlokosewitschii*) and the lipstick-shaped buds are already visible at the base. I count them, remembering vaguely how many there were the year before, and feel satisfied that this year they are fatter and more plentiful. The crowns are now surrounded by self-sown *Tulipa sprengeri*, which is naturalizing so successfully among them that I make a point of mulching here first while the tulips are still dormant. An upturned plastic pot is carefully placed over the shoots of the peonies so that they are not damaged in the process, the compost forked around the crown, and the pot finally pulled free to reveal the shoots. This is a method that is also ideal for perennials such as *Achillea*, which resent the mulch immediately around their crowns.

Buds of *Paeonia mlokosewitschii*.

The Turkish knife and a pair of secateurs are my tools of choice. Some perennials, like the *Molinia caerulea* subsp. *arundinacea* 'Transparent', yield when the timing is right because they have already rotted where last year's growth meets the crown. A gentle tug is all that is needed, but you should never yank too hard for fear of breaking away some of the living crown. Old growth that resists is cut as close to the base as possible without damaging the new shoots.

Some perennials will quite happily hold last year's growth well into the next season, but you don't want to be cutting back the fennel and damaging the delicate new foliage by leaving it until the new growth is up and started. I always cut the old stems of the woodier perennials to the base of the plant, otherwise you will leave behind a series of jagged pegs concealed beneath the summer foliage, which catch you while you are weeding. I know if I have done the job right when I run a springbok rake over the beds to catch the remains that I've missed when hand-picking – it is easy to make the pass without snaring the tines.

All too often I find myself making the last sweep with the rake at the end of the day, as it will have been a busy one, stooping and cutting and ferrying thatch to the compost heap. Dim light is the worst light for checking over the beds, but a final sweep is worth it before the end of play. A second sweep reveals seedling sycamores that were camouflaged until now and buttercups lurking in the newly cleared crowns. Another look also reveals perennials that have died out in the centre and need splitting, as well as plants that I had all but forgotten and are in danger of being trampled unless marked clearly with a cane.

Dicentra, Trillium, Veratrum and lilies will be ruined if you stray into an area that appears to be unoccupied. You will never forget the terrible crunch if it happens to you – a year's growth lost in a hasty second.

Over the course of February, I strip the garden back until the newly filled compost heap is as full as the beds are empty. Although I have grown to like the shock of the new and tolerate the naked fences, friends who visit at this time cannot believe that this is the same garden they sat out in the summer. 'What have you done with the garden? Where's it all gone?', they ask. In no time, though, the compost heap starts to collapse and there is a countermovement in the beds. Crimson fingers on the *Geranium* 'Patricia' (Brempat) the spears of *Narcissus* 'Jenny' and the first opium poppy seedlings appear to break the manacles of winter.

Ground Cover

I dislike seeing bare soil in the garden. It looks unnatural and I aim for it to be covered, like a forest floor. Bare soil appears on the allotment and in the vegetable beds when I am cultivating, but even there I like to sow close so that the herbs and vegetables knit to strangle weeds under their canopy. Exposed soil also appears in the beds from time to time around new plantings or broadcast seed that likes open ground. Opium poppies and the Californian poppies (*Eschscholzia californica*) are pioneers and need new territory.

The forest floor is a metaphor, but when the garden is stripped to the bone, it is an image that I like to use as a touchstone. Under the shade of the trees and shrubs, where the soil is protected, the image is easy to retain, but out in the open it is still important to keep the principle alive. A deciduous wood rarely goes from canopy to nothing at ground level, and I approach the perennial planting as if it were a wood, with a natural ascendance of layers. The lofty summer perennials rise up to form the canopy, but they do so through a series of layers that terminates with ground cover. In the better parts of the garden, where I have cracked the combinations, I am happy to find that there is very little naked ground once the garden is cleared and, where it does appear, it is a continual refining process to build up a community that will cover it. Every plant has an appropriate bedfellow if you look hard enough.

The best ground-covering plants tend to be evergreen and content in shade. The likes of *Symphytum ibericum* and *Luzula sylvatica* are also tolerant of dry conditions once they are established, but they are too strong and invasive for this garden. I work with plants that are less prone to uninhibited spreading. *Tellima grandiflora* 'Purpurteppich' colours a rich burgundy in the winter and can be used to sweep under deciduous woody companions such as the shrub roses. In winter, the leaves of the *Tellima* are green overlaid with plum but, in April, a myriad of wire-thin stems appear above them. In this variety, these are as dark as charcoal and beaded with tiny, fringed bells, which are a pale spring green and shimmer in sunshine. This is one of the best forms for the richness of foliage, but it does not have the perfume of the Odorata Group.

Evergreen *Epimedium* and the shiny-leaved *Asarum europaeum* are also clump-forming but, once the clumps meet, the cover that they provide is complete and anything planted to emerge through them needs to have the deep-rooted stamina of hellebores or a well-established peony. Creeping evergreens such as *Vinca minor* and the semi-evergreen *Geranium macrorrhizum* need to be carefully weeded around while they are knitting together, as do all ground-covering plants if they are to do their job effectively. For ground cover to work, it needs to be given the good start that any other plant would, despite the fact that this is often the layer that you take for granted later.

The most adaptable ground-covering plants will be happy to fall into the shade of taller companions as long as the canopy is not too dense in the summer. But not all have to keep their foliage in the winter to do the job effectively. Dense summer perennials, such as the *Geranium* 'Patricia' or the *Hemerocallis* 'Stafford', also shade the soil in the growing months. Although they retreat to nothing from November to March, the gap they leave behind can be plugged with bulbs that will take advantage of the season during which they lie dormant. The *Ranunculus ficaria* 'Brazen Hussy' and the snowdrops are up by the time the foliage of the geranium has been pulled into the ground and they will have completed their life cycles by the time the crimson shoots of 'Patricia' have turned into foliage. Bare patches between deciduous perennials are filled with these early opportunists, and even though some of the bulbs will not flower until later, they are covering naked ground and provide interest while they are feeding their storage organs.

I also use ground cover wherever there is an edge that needs softening. Edges and boundaries are a constant in London, so I cushion the meeting points between path and bed, bed and terrace, and let the cracks in the terrace fill with mind-your-own-business. In the shade of the extension, the *Soleirolia* softens the paving joints like moss. Out in the sun, the forest floor metaphor continues with plants that spill out low into the open, as they might on the edge of the woodland. The likes of *Erigeron karvinskianus* and *Viola labradorica* are ideal, as they are self-seeding opportunists and happiest finding their own place. Plant them where you want them to be and they invariably migrate to an area that is borderline. And so, I let them creep into the slate, so that the edges of the path are fringed and made that much less clear-cut. Open space here is hard space, but the soil is always protected.

'Brazen Hussy'

The liquorice foliage of the *Ranunculus ficaria* 'Brazen Hussy' is up while the rest of the garden is still slumbering. It's dark enough to be barely visible against the naked earth, and I have to remember to pull away last year's spent foliage to give them room to breathe. They build a flat rosette over the space of a couple of months, one leaf on top of the next, lying flat to catch all of the available light. The buds gather in strength and are visible by early March, and the first few flowers spring open just as the snowdrops are going over. This is triggered by a bright sunlit day and, despite their tiny stature, you can see the flowers from inside the house. The leaves are shiny, almost blue-black in sunshine as they reflect the sky. The flowers are glossy as silk. They are gold, pure and unadulterated, the embodiment of the changing season.

Foliage of *Ranunculus ficaria* 'Brazen Hussy'.

I cannot remember where my original plants came from, but I carried them around in a terracotta pan from garden to garden. For the twenty or more years that I have grown them, I have never tired of their lust for life and, without fail, they have returned each spring to prove their dependability. By nature they are woodlanders, up early as soon as the days lengthen in order to harvest all the available light, and gone by the time the canopy closes over in early summer. When we moved here, I liberated them from their congested pan and they now line both sides of the path with yellow, and I have planted mahogany-backed *Crocus* 'Gipsy Girl' to join them. Getting them to spread has taken some time, dividing and redividing the clumps, like the snowdrops, just after the flowers fade. The plants are easily pulled apart and, in the window between the last flowers and dormancy, they get the foothold they need to come back vigorously the following season. Their only enemy, as far as I have found, is the pigeons, which some years peck relentlessly at the corms as the plants are just emerging. Netting them until there is other food available has been enough to foil their dinner plans.

Christopher Lloyd selected and named 'Brazen Hussy' as a sport of the green-leaved celandines that grow in the woods below Great Dixter. I have seen them there myself, blooming with primroses and then bluebells, the black sheep among the flock of green. He named this sport very brilliantly, for they push on brazenly, despite the inhospitable March weather. The best plants are always those that get the sunshine and, like the crocus, they need the light for their flowers to open to their full potential. I have the equally lovely but more demure, dark-leaved form called 'Jake Perry', with creamy flowers, at the front of the house. Every year I mean to move it so that it gets more light but I would not want to get it close to its golden cousin for fear of cross-pollinating.

Now that the 'Brazen Hussy' have established themselves, they are proving they like it by seeding. Seedlings take about three years to flower, but as occasional seedlings have reverted to green, I make sure these are winkled out before they mature. The true *Ranunculus ficaria* can be a menace in the wrong place because its tiny tubers break and rebreak as they increase. This is never a problem among shrubs and strong perennials, which think nothing of coming up through them, as their foliage is gone by early summer.

Spring Sowing

Some time in late February or early March, the weather warms enough for the first seeds to start germinating. These tiny pinpricks of green are the bravest and most capable of dealing with the unreliable weather, but it is movement nonetheless and always heart-warming. The first to break dormancy are the opium poppies, with two hair-like cotyledons of pale grey-green. They represent the opportunistic hardy annuals that like to get their feet down early. You will not see much action above ground, but the tiny taproot is delving deep so that, by the time the weather warms, they are ready to get themselves ahead of the crowd. On the allotment, the calendulas are doing much the same where they self-sowed last year, and I know that, as soon as they have cast off the empty seed case and thrown their first leaves back to catch the light, the touchpaper has been lit.

It is the days lengthening, as much as the temperature of the soil rising to 6°C (43°F), that make this possible. That and a guaranteed supply of moisture mean it's worthwhile sowing a few of the hardiest plants. Fairy Wings poppies, *Eschscholzia* and a little wild rocket in the salad beds can be established early, but it is best to wait until the end of March before committing more to the soil without protection. Whether it comes in like a lion and goes out like a lamb, or in like a lamb and out like a lion, March is always a month that will see adversity, and most seed can wait.

The first seedlings breaking ground are the catalyst for getting out the seed box. There are half-hardy annuals that need six to eight weeks growing time ahead of the last frost to flower well in our climate, and a range of vegetables that can soon be sown under the protection of the cloches. I lay the seed out in an arc on the kitchen table like a pack of cards. Of those that need to be sown inside, the slowest-growing *Cleome hassleriana* (syn. *spinosa*) are put to the left. These will be sown first, followed by *Nicotiana* and so on, with the faster-growing *Tagetes* and tomatoes to the right. I know from trial and error that the last week of February is the ideal time to start the slower seedlings, as their germination alone can take two to three weeks. The faster-growing *Ipomaea lobata* and *Tagetes* 'Cinnabar' will be up in no time, so they are left for at least a month, otherwise they will become drawn and etiolated.

As I have limited space, the seed is sown in small pots, a pinch, no more. Mastering seed distribution is crucial for the seedlings not to rot off through overcrowding. This is the only time I ever use peat-based compost and I use it in such small quantities that I have convinced myself this is acceptable. Unfortunately, in my experience, it has proven to be the best and most reliable compost for germination but I continue to try the alternatives and use a coir-based compost to grow things on. I dampen the soil with a rose prior to sowing. When the seedlings are large enough to transplant, they are liberated into a more sustainable growing medium. Pots are also cleaned prior to sowing to diminish the chances of fungal attack.

The size of the seed bears little relation, it seems, to its parent. The giant *Nicotiana sylvestris* has seed like dust, while *N. suaveolens*, its slighter cousin, has seed the size of a pinhead. The finest seed is left on the surface of the compost rather than covered. As a general rule of thumb, larger seed is covered with compost to twice its depth. I have an old sieve that distributes a fine dusting of compost. The pots are labelled and covered with glass or cling film to keep the compost damp and conditions stable. I turn this covering daily to avoid an excessive build-up of condensation.

I start off all of my seedlings in the house, right by the southwest-facing windows at the back. For the first week, I move the *Cleome* from inside to outside during the day, as the fluctuating temperature breaks their dormancy. Everything else is happy to remain in the warmth. I like the close observation that follows, and it takes me back to my childhood, watching and willing the seeds to break the surface. Without fail, germination always brings with it a feeling of optimism, but it is important to catch it early and move the seedlings into the lightest position so that they do not strain for light. Long stems are prone to rotting off, so you want your seedlings sturdy.

Growing seedlings in the house is far from ideal, and one day I will have a greenhouse to save the inconvenience of the juggling act that ensues. The first few weeks are easy while I have as many pots as there are varieties but, as soon as they have produced their first true leaves, the seedlings need to be carefully divided and put into an individual container or tray. They look horribly vulnerable in your hand but, as long as they are only ever picked up by the first cotyledons, they will survive transplanting. Picking a seedling up by the stem is the equivalent of a stranglehold and will cause irreparable damage.

I keep the spare seedlings as backup, returning them to the pot for a couple of weeks just in case the transplanted ones fail, but I have learned to pot up only as many as I need, to save having them in every room of the house. By the middle of April, I risk putting the most mature and the hardiest out into the cold frame, where they will be covered with fleece and grown on into early May. It is a relief to get them outside and to have the windowsills back. You can see the relief in the seedlings, too, as they fill out in readiness for the summer ahead.

Hellebores and Snowdrops

My affinity with shade-lovers comes from my early experiences of gardening in woodland, where I got to know the rhythms that are particular to this environment. The light filtered through the canopy to bathe the woodland floor in milky shadows during the winter, and you could feel the spring gathering energy as the race began. The season was fast and furious, and the early-to-rise plants knew that they needed to get their growing done early. Once the trees were in growth and the canopy closed over, the trees robbed the root-infested ground of moisture and the forest floor of light. To garden the shade successfully, I learned to ride these extremes and I grew to love the things that thrived there as much for their delicate form as for their tenacity.

The whole of the left-hand side of the garden is influenced by shade. The towering extension runs into the fence, which slips behind the hornbeam to join the tall wall of the garages at the end. For the whole winter, the garden is split in two, with sun to the right of the path, and shade in most of the left, until the sun swings around in the afternoon to break the spell with evening light. I have to think with one hat to the sunny side and with another where it is cool and find ways for the planting to feel homogeneous and not divided in two. It really helps to think that this garden might be on the edge of woodland, with the cooling influence of the interior and sunlight and airiness beyond.

I am lucky with my shade because everywhere it is without the drying influence of tree roots, except for the hornbeam's. Neighbours' trees are far enough away for us to get the benefit of the backdrop without the downside of the roots. This means I can grow a wide range of plants because, in general, the shade remains damp and cool in the summer. Moisture-loving *Trillium*, ferns, *Paris* and the Asian *Epimedium* usually sulk in the microclimate of London, but I can indulge them where the air is cool.

Pink Picotee form of *Helleborus orientalis*.

Although I love the hornbeam, the *Cytisus battandieri*, which provided the shade there before, was better for the plants that grew in its influence. Despite its modest appearance, the hornbeam is hungry, with a dense network of fibrous roots and a ceiling of foliage that is fairly opaque in terms of what could be considered dappled shade. Dappled shade and a non-invasive root system are the ideal combination for planting partners, but I have had to adapt as the hornbeam has gathered in strength. In drought, I now have to drench the *Hydrangea aspera* Villosa Group, which grows in the hornbeam's shade and, as the hydrangea leans further towards the light, I have to keep an eye on the 'Late Windflower' peony to ensure it is not smothered beneath it. The pool of cool under the tree keeps the garden feeling dynamic, but it will ultimately limit the range of plants that will grow beneath it and I am ever mindful that it is an area prone to sudden change as the tree increases in bulk.

Galanthus 'Magnet'.

The snowdrops are the first to emerge in this area and they make the most of the moisture that is still in the ground. Every other December, I tip a barrowload of compost around the hydrangea and this has been distributed by the blackbirds by the time the bulbs are up. The dark foil suits the snowdrops and they lift this corner of the garden in February with dazzling, weather-defeating flower. I have a good form of *Galanthus nivalis* that originally came as in-the-green plants through the post. I bought a hundred initially and planted them in groups of five in a drift, which I have extended over the years. It takes about three or four years for them to bulk up enough to divide, which I do immediately after they have flowered, as they move best if given a few weeks to settle in before dormancy. Dry snowdrop bulbs are far more prone to rotting, though the wide-leaved *G. elwesii* is an exception to the rule.

I resisted getting to know the named varieties of *Galanthus* in the belief that a good form of the standard *G. nivalis* was all I needed but, one February, I came upon the Snowdrop Theatre at the Chelsea Physic Garden. Looking at the plants close up and together, I could clearly see the subtle differences between them. These drive the engine of galanthophile obsession, and I succumbed to buying a few plants to see if they would be good in the garden. *Galanthus* 'Magnet' is distinctive for its large flowers and knitting-needle eye where the pedicel holds the bud at the top of the stem. Its height makes it a fine thing in the breeze, and the flowers dance on a blustery day. *Galanthus* 'S. Arnott' is as well formed as any snowdrop can be and has a delicate perfume when picked and brought inside. A hint of warmth makes them fling their petals back like outstretched arms, so it is worth putting a few in the sun to see this joyous reaction.

Galanthus 'Alison Hilary'.

A few years ago, the garden writer Tania Compton sent me a solitary bulb of *G.* 'Galatea' and it has bulked up and doubled with every year in the ground. It has the stature and stamina of an athlete, and I think that might be a good thing, despite the fact that the charm of a snowdrop is usually its diminutive size. However, I will not become a galanthophile, and am happy with just a handful. All I require is that each is distinctive enough to tell them apart when planted in a crowd.

In a good year, the snowdrops and the lenten roses come together, though I must admit to the hellebores doing less well as this area becomes more densely planted. I think this has as much to do with the *Persicaria* shading them out in the late summer as the influence of the hornbeam roots. *Helleborus* × *hybridus* is happy in shade but it likes good living, and I suspect that the combination of shade and summer drought are having their influence. Even so, they do well enough because there is moisture in the ground early in the year when they are growing. March would not be the same without them, and I have put together a dozen or so plants from favourites that I have come across over the years.

Black Form of *Helleborus orientalis*.

The darkest of them is a deep plum-purple, with a dusting of bloom on the outside and a darker interior. Although I have not fallen out of love with them – it is hard not to fall in love with the lenten roses – the dark forms are not the easiest to use. The addition of the snowdrops among them is important because the contrast of the light with the dark means that they do not get lost. I have also introduced a good clean white and a lime-green form, which has a delicate and complex freckled interior. The greens are very subtle and a personal favourite. One day, I plan to team them up with some good yellows.

I have learned from experience to seek out the best hellebores when they are in flower, as they are hugely variable when grown from seed.

Removed from the main group, because it has quite a different mood, is a good picotee form. The original plant has now seeded, and ten or so seedlings were gathered up after they had germinated at the base of the mother plant. They are quite variable but all have degrees of distinctive veining, the white base overlaid with cherry-coloured markings that look as if the edges of the petals have been dipped in ink. For some reason, this form is a little later to bloom, but never so late that flowers can't be picked and added to a selection for the house. Plucking single flowers and laying them in a shallow bowl of water keeps them in good condition for two to three days and allows you the pleasure of seeing what is often the best of the markings in the upturned flower.

When the plants are young, I leave the old foliage in the belief that it is needed to feed the new growth. However, as the plants become established, I remove it as soon as I see the flowers emerging at the crown. The plants look cleaner this way and are less prone to developing disease if they are given a clean start at the beginning of their growing season.

PAGE 101
Papaver somniferum germinating in last year's pod.

Spring

Mulch and Weeding

I am a devotee of mulching, and I hate to see the soil naked and exposed
to the elements. Take a look at any natural setting and you will find
the soil is protected in one way or another – an eiderdown of fallen
leaves in woodland, moss in the shade and, out in the open, it is rare
for vegetation not to have shielded it from the elements. A natural
covering prevents soil from drying in the sun, wind and rain, from
leaching essential nutrients and from compaction of the surface.
When it is shielded and protected, soil will remain stable, with an
even temperature and moisture content, providing just the right
conditions for the beneficial organisms that keep it alive and fertile.

Although I have mulched for as long as I can remember, with
whatever suitable material there has been to hand, I do it less
frequently now that the garden is established and there is less ground
exposed when the perennials are cleared. In the early years, it was an
annual exercise at the end of the winter because the plants were young
and the exposed soil between them was more extensive. Mulching
kept the weeds down, and there were plenty as the seed bank was
turned during the initial cultivation but, ten years on, the majority
of the seedlings are now garden plants.

The opportunistic seeders are what keep the garden feeling free
and relaxed, but I have to exercise a controlling hand to keep the
planting in balance. Out in the sun, the *Verbena bonariensis* and
Eryngium giganteum appear in their thousands. As I need only a
handful of each, I work through the borders with a hand-fork not

PAGE 106
New season's compost.

long after the garden is cleared, ensuring that they don't choke the star performers. The *Dierama*, in particular, hate competition and will quickly sulk and dwindle if their bases are crowded. There are a few plants that could also become a menace. If the *Smyrnium perfoliatum* were left to its own devices, it would soon establish a new status quo in the shady areas. As it is a biennial, I keep on top of it by removing the majority of the lime-green flowers before they seed, but still I have to judge carefully the number that I leave in place. You need only a handful of plants to provide the froth of green required at *Allium* time, and it is a brute if it decides it likes you. The *Stylophorum lasiocarpum* is also a prolific interloper. They are happy to live in the shade of other plants while they are developing but, once they get a foothold, they are surprisingly thuggish and will muscle out their neighbours like a cuckoo in the nest. If you get to them while they are young, they are easy to pull out.

Some less aggressive self-seeders can be more or less left to their own devices. The maroon seedlings of *Euphorbia dulcis* 'Chameleon', which I introduced in a very early incarnation of the garden, come up all over the garden every spring, although the parent plants, affected by rust, died out almost immediately. The acid yellow and pure orange of the poppies *Meconopsis cambrica* and *Papaver rupifragum* are almost never unwelcome, wherever they choose to appear because they are so light on their feet.

Certain seedlings are left in place because they either make superior plants when self-sown, have a short life cycle or are better while they are youngsters. The *Alcea rugosa* develop rust in their third year and, for that reason, they are given a chance to regenerate naturally. I keep a rotation of seedlings going so that the plants are always youthful. The *Cephalaria dipsacoides* is also proving itself to be an unreliable perennial here but a fairly prolific seeder, and the seedlings flower in their second year, covering for the older plants, which tend to rot off during the winter.

Weeding is an important exercise this early in the year, and if I manage to deal with the seedlings before the perennials around them close over, I won't have to do it again. I do two sweeps every two weeks or so before I mulch the areas that need it, and then around the time I stake, to avoid stepping on the soil repeatedly. Mulching ground that is already infested with perennial weeds is pointless and will only improve growing conditions and promote their vigour. I make an annual foray with a border fork to winkle out the troublesome roots where I know they are a problem and let them dry in the sun before consigning them to the bin.

When the weeding is done, I mulch on rotation, moving from one area to the next, in a three-year cycle. I find this is enough to keep the soil fertility up, and it gives the self-seeders a chance to develop communities where I want them. I use my garden compost carefully, as it is difficult to get a heap hot enough to break down all the seeds that go into it. The compost regularly sprouts *Nicotiana*, tomatoes, evening primrose, opium poppies, as well as a host of other things. This is fine where you can easily weed them out or where plants are dense enough to shade the seedlings out, but it defeats the object if you are looking for your beds to be clean in the summer. If mulch is to perform its function without adding another job in the process, it should be free of seeds and weeds.

Composted bark, mushroom compost and recycled green waste are available bagged and are easy to haul through the garage. I used cocoa shell for the first few years here, but found the sticky impenetrable mat it created too much for many plants to struggle through. If you can get it, well-rotted manure is good around the roses, and the woodland areas never look more authentic than when mulched with leaf mould. A mulched garden will never look neater than when you have just done it – turned down and tucked in and ready for the growing season.

Spring Bulbs

The cold frame has been closed for the last three months to protect the overwintering cuttings and early bulbs. I have opened it a chink when the weather has been mild, to let in the air and to check on the watering, as the pots do get dry even in winter sunshine. Life in this two square metres keeps me hopeful. By the end of February, I am checking the frame weekly, as the *Iris reticulata* can run to flower in a couple of days once the buds are visible. The early spears bring more joy than you are ever really prepared for, and I ferry the pots up to the house to observe their progress at close quarters on the basement windowsill.

Every moment counts this early in the year, and the iris are as good in bud as they are when open. Tapering like a dart, the overlay of petals intensifies the colour where the petals are scrolled together. My childhood friend Geraldine taught me the joy of growing them in pots and she used to bring them into the house where they would last only a week. Mine are kept outside, unless there are enough to pick to add to a winter posy of snowdrops, and there they last a fortnight or more, depending upon the weather.

Narcissus 'Jenny', *N.* 'Jack Snipe' and *N.* 'Canaliculatus'.

Suddenly, when your back is turned, the petals throw themselves back to the horizontal and the buds are gone. *Iris histrioides* 'George' is the darkest of those that I have on the go at the moment, a royal purple, with gold on the falls. *Iris* 'George' (Reticulata) smells of primroses and is the finest flowered of the three, a true sky-blue with white and dark denim-blue on the lower petals. *Iris* 'Katharine Hodgkin' (Reticulata) is palest blue-green, a curious colour that is odd in open ground. Up close in a pan, you can savour the dark inky splashes that overlay the gold on the falls. The petals are delicately striped to concentrate the colour, and fade to a ghostly blue at the outer rim as if to make the pool of colour hover.

During the time that the iris are out, the garden comes to life. The *Crocus tommasinianus* are the first to stir, rising from the dirt in the giant pot under the *Cercis canadensis* 'Forest Pansy' in just a week. This self-sowing species is taller than most and draws itself up here towards the light. Its position is a little too shady for it because, of all the spring flowers, it requires sunshine to make it throw open its flowers. The buds are the palest 'mother-of-pearl' as the three outer petals that form the bud cover the darker colour within. When they open, the inner petals are shot with bright lilac and they fade towards a pale centre that keeps them feeling light and provides a shocking contrast to the tangerine stamens, stigma and style. Bring a bud inside and it will open before your very eyes in the warmth.

The rest of the crocus are in pots and are relayed from the frame as they come to life. I am working through the extensive list of *Crocus chrysanthus*, which I love for the difference between the inside of the flower and the outside. With their frequently striped, marked or bi-coloured exterior, they are like two flowers, one closed, the other open. The best make it into the beds, though the birds tear them to pieces further away from the house if they are not protected. I wonder if this would be the case if they were in grass and with more around them as a distraction. My favourites, after trial and error, are 'Gypsy Girl', 'Zwanenberg Bronze', 'Cream Beauty' and 'Snow Bunting'.

Beth Chatto once gave me some *Narcissus pallidiflorus* with the story that the artist Cedric Morris had given them to her from a collection he had made in the wild. Connections like this are extremely special and the plants remain an early favourite. They are distinctive for their precociousness and for the way that the buds face the sky before tilting a few degrees to flower. They are an elegant pale primrose-yellow and about the size of a Tenby daffodil. I am running a little trial of the small-flowered hybrids so that I can retain the best for the beds and know what I am letting loose in their thousands on

Iris 'George'.

Narcissus 'W. P. Milner'.

my clients' properties. The *Narcissus cyclamineus* hybrids, the named jonquils and *N. triandrus* hybrids are by far my favourites because I prefer the smaller flowers and the fine, grassy foliage. This is easily worked in among perennials and is almost invisible in a meadow. The finer leaves disappear when the flowers fade and I think they are superior to the larger-flowering hybrids, which leave behind a jumble of straps and tangles.

'Jack Snipe', 'February Gold' and 'February Silver' are some of the earliest, while I love 'Jenny' for the way the flowers change as they age. The first few days see the trumpets go from palest primrose to a chalky white, and they are distinctive for the reflexed petals that are thrown back in a stretch. I have recently got to know 'W. P. Milner', another pale-flowered form, which retains something of the species about it. The smaller-flowered 'Hawera' has several flowers to a stem and comes a bit later in April. 'Pipit' has heavily scented flowers in a soft, bright yellow that fades to a frosted white in the trumpet. The jonquils are good for their slightly later flower and the intensity of colour and perfume. I prefer gold when it can be dotted through a planting rather than appearing like a rash this early in the year.

Not all the *Narcissus* are easy. I lost my true Tenby daffodils to narcissus fly, which, interestingly enough, is rarely a problem in shade, and this seems to be the only thing you can do to protect against it. So far, it hasn't struck again elsewhere. Against the odds, I persist in trying to get *Narcissus tazetta* to thrive – I love the early flower and the intensity of the perfume when I am blessed with the occasional bloom. They hail from dry, arid regions, and I bake them in a hot spot after flowering and then move their pots into the garage when they are dormant, to emulate a dry summer. For scent and early flower, 'Scilly White' have proven far more reliable.

For a while, I grew *Fritillaria imperialis* among the *Hemerocallis* 'Stafford', but they were consistently decimated by the first wave of lily beetles. In the end, I took them out, as they were constantly being stripped by the grubs. The lily beetles also like the snakeshead fritillaries, but I keep a few in the special woodland corner close to the path, where they are easier to pick over. *Fritillaria meleagris* remains one of my favourites and there are two clumps here, thriving where the ground is dampest. For some reason, the white form is doing rather better than its plum-coloured chequered siblings and they are starting to seed among the ferns, establishing a little colony on their own. They are light enough on their feet to arc through the perennials in this area and seem happy to be consumed as soon as spring gathers pace. Such grace and good behaviour are so very welcome.

Narcissus 'Jenny'.

Fritillaria meleagris.

Light

The light has been gradually building towards the spring equinox, with the shadow of the house retreating daily on the fence at the end. When the clocks change a week or so later, it feels as if you have been given a bonus, and we are out there pottering until it gets too dark to see. It is intrinsic to the garden's character that it faces west, and the evenings are the best time when the sun swings around low and everything is backlit. We have the best of both worlds here, with sun at the front until nearly lunchtime and a back garden long enough for there to be a sunny breakfast spot at the end in the mornings, too. The orientation is much gentler than if we were to face north/south. A blaze on one side and cool, relentless shade on the other would make for two spaces far more split in their character.

I spent the best part of a year working out where the hot spots were and where I would have to work with the shade. We are overshadowed only by the beech tree in the garden of the neighbours behind us, and I have purposely introduced shade on the middle deck with the hornbeam to create a pool of darkness that you can head for at the end of the path. The extension casts its shadow across the whole terrace until the sun swings around in the afternoon. By that time, though, the garden is bathed in light along its length and the sun is captured in the enclosure. After a hot summer's day, the heat is held on the terrace well into the evening by the dark paving and brick walls. As you move out and beyond the terrace, you venture into noticeably cooler air.

Contrast is important, and moving from light to shade, warm to cool, is key to the rhythm of the garden as you move through it. Shadow provides another opportunity to see plants in silhouette, the dappling of the hornbeam on the deck, the jagged shadow patterns of the bamboo on the stone of the terrace. Shade provides tranquillity, while light gives energy, and the sunnier areas are where colour tends to work best and can be used most freely. I do use colour in the shade, with the luminous magenta of *Geranium* 'Patricia' and deep royal purple of *Aconitum* 'Spark's Variety', but the hot colours become hotter when fully lit. I save the fiercest colours for the bed next to the deck because south light falls directly onto the planting as you sit with your back to the sun under the leafy hornbeam. My least favourite time for looking at gardens is when the summer sun is highest in the sky, but it works here in the middle of the day, with the colour pulsing at you as you sit in the cool, deep shade.

I like the way in which the light here changes so dramatically throughout the day and how we move around the garden to make the

PAGE 113
Early spring sunshine on the neighbour's ash tree.

PAGES 114–15
Catkins on the hornbeam.

PAGES 116–17
Crocus tommasinianus underneath the *Cercis canadensis*.

PAGES 118–19
Pruning during April showers.

most of it. I have learned to play with the light so that it brings out the best in every part of the garden, and the afternoon backlighting has informed how the plants are placed to best effect. The pleated leaves of the *Crocosmia* 'Lucifer' are their greatest asset this early in the year, and backlighting turns neon the lime-green daggers emerging from dark earth. In summer, silken seedheads of *Stipa barbata* twist and float like flaxen hair, while every outline of *Eryngium giganteum* is picked out in a jagged silver halo.

The *Cercis canadensis* 'Forest Pansy' is the best example of a plant that comes alive when given the right lighting. When the evenings begin to open out, the dark, angular branches are studded with tiny flowers, which turn a crackling mauve in the afternoon sunlight. The heart-shaped foliage returns soon after the flowering, and the embryonic leaves are a ruby-red when filled with light. A bright summer afternoon sees the whole plant ablaze, and it seems to pulse, as full of life as anything can be.

Flowers on the *Cercis canadensis* 'Forest Pansy'

Tulips

I find strong colour easier to handle in pots than fixed in the beds at this point in the year, but I try not to be precious about it, in the belief that it is welcome in any form after a winter of monochrome. Tulips feature strongly here but the majority of the large-flowered hybrids never seem to last long-term, often lost to ground slugs and summer wet, and returning as nothing more than foliage. They are cheap enough to indulge in a hundred of each and I treat them like annuals, discarding them after they have flowered. In truth, I rarely have the heart to do this immediately, so some of the pots contain new bulbs, while those saved from last year are kept to test the most reliable varieties. The spicily sherbet-scented 'Ballerina' make it into the display every year, as they always flower again in their second year. After that, I replace them with a new batch.

'Abu Hassan' has proven to be a firm favourite, with its dark mahogany flowers fringed with flame-yellow along the edges. They are strong, upright and unbelievably showy when the sun comes out, and they unfurl to reveal their golden throats. The lily-flowered 'West Point' completely changes its character in sunshine, the tight-lipped tapers flinging themselves wide open with complete abandon to form a chrome-yellow star, which closes again as the light moves off them. Yellow is always easy in spring and particularly welcome after a dim winter.

Tulipa 'Ballerina' and 'West Point'.

PAGE 120
Tulipa sylvestris.

I have enjoyed the 'Attila' tulips but I had to move them up to the terrace to enjoy them on their own. The lilac flowers were just too strong and brazen, and competed with the delicate growth of its neighbours. Of the species, the named varieties of *Tulipa clusiana* have been some of the best, short-flowering if they hit a warm week but elegant on long stems and delightful for their bi-colouring, with one tone outside and another inside, revealed when they fling their flowers open in sunshine. You have to like surprises if you are experimenting, and the varieties that I either decide I don't like or choose for cutting are brought into the house to be enjoyed in a jug, simply for themselves and in another context.

Tulipa 'Sapporro'.

Although they dwindle within a year in the ground, I have continued to work a hundred 'Sapporro' in among the *Narcissus* 'Jenny'. I originally grew the lily-flowered 'White Triumphator' in this position to capture the moment when the catkins are hanging in the hornbeam but, one year, the wrong bulbs were supplied. I tracked down their true name, 'Sapporro', because it soon became clear to me that I liked 'Sapporro' more. It has all the poise and elegance of its white-flowered cousin, but I find it infinitely superior. As it rises tall above the soft coppery growth of the *Actaea* (formally known as *Cimicifuga*), the buds are a soft primrose-yellow but, over the space of a few days, the colour slowly drains from the petals, shifting to a beautiful bone-white. In a cool spring, this transformation can take the best part of a fortnight and the flowers last three weeks, so they bridge the end of *Narcissus* and the beginning of the *Allium*.

I grow two species tulips that are reliable in the beds. Both prefer damp conditions, though the starry yellow *Tulipa sylvestris* likes the sun. I have it growing through the glossy early foliage of *Ferula tingitana* 'Cedric Morris', and the tilted buds open only when the sun shines. They splay in a yolky salutation that faces into the sun, so careful placing is required to get the best of them. *Tulipa sprengeri* hold off flowering until well into May, and they are the last of the tulips to flower. I started with twelve flowering bulbs, which have self-sown happily. Although the bulbs are expensive, an investment in a couple will pay dividends in little more than three years. They enjoyed the shade of the coyote willows while they were still standing, and seem happy to break the rules as far as tulips go. As long as they get the early spring sunshine while the perennials are still under ground, they come back with a vengeance in this corner of the garden. The flowers are sparse, and open to a wonderful clear scarlet edged with gold. I love the violent flash of them when they break through the greenery burgeoning around them.

Tulipa sprengeri.

Control

As the days lengthen, you can practically see the garden moving. The fact that you are low down when you are on the terrace heightens the effect of the beds filling out and ascending. The *Eryngium agavifolium* provide the first evidence of this upward motion as the new leaves push away vertically from the base. The jagged edges are almost transparent this early in the year, and their silhouette appears to have a halo around it picked out in light. The flowering stems emerge shortly afterwards as if they are being drawn from the ground by invisible threads. The *Nectaroscordum siculum*, which are woven among them, have sent up their flowering stems in much the same movement. The buds are visible within the papery tapers at the top, and there is a moment of tension in the days before they open. When the tunic is cast aside, the dusky bruised purple bells fall from their upward position, and the bees are among them in no time. They hang heavily until they are pollinated, when they rise up again to form the seed cases.

Stakes around the emerging foliage of *Lilium henryi*.

The ground plane is swelling fast while this is happening, with the perennials gathering strength in readiness for a bolt skyward. It will be no time at all until it becomes too difficult to wade into the beds, and I work through one more time with the border fork to clear any weeds that will soon be in hiding when the foliage closes over. Now is the time to exercise control because things can go horribly wrong by the middle of summer if they are not set up properly early on.

The flush of opium poppy seedlings is a good example, and I leave them until now to seed around in the gaps between the permanent residents. They never come up in the same place from one year to the next, and I like this element of chance. In truth, you need only a dozen plants, and no more than one or two in each position, otherwise they crowd each other out. Their opportunistic behaviour is never particularly neighbourly, and you have to watch like a hawk if they are not to overwhelm a weaker plant, such as the *Iris chrysographes* or the *Gillenia trifoliata*, in their determination to set seed. By July, once they have achieved their goal, their foliage will be browning, each plant a shadow of itself. If you have managed this well, the gap they leave behind will be consumed without a hitch.

You only have to look at the list of plants that I am growing here to see how much is shoehorned into a relatively small space and, for things not to splay more than they should, they need to be cajoled into growing how I want them to. The art of keeping the look as free and naturalistic as possible lies in careful staking. Without it, the garden would be behaving like a drunken crowd by the middle of August.

The hollyhocks would have toppled, preventing the later-flowering *Salvia guaranitica* behind them from getting the light they need, while the *Lilium henryi* would be arching to touch the ground. The arch in the stems of the *L. henryi* is one of the things particular about it, but the flowers often hang on the stems too heavily. In a larger garden, the splaying *Crocosmia* 'Lucifer' and the lean on the *Persicaria polymorpha* could be tolerated, but I am demanding a lot in a small space and it needs restraint in order to work.

Control is something I exercise only at strategic moments and only when it is needed. Now is the moment to set up those perennials that need support. The *Aconitum* 'Spark's Variety' in the shade of the hydrangea are drawn up more than they would be in a sunnier spot, and I need to catch them early while the growth is still forming. Once they tumble and try to right themselves, it is too late and they never perform as well. In addition to staking, and once they are about knee height, I administer the 'Chelsea Chop' to the later-flowering perennials. Tipping out encourages branching and stockiness, and the leggy *Ageratina altissima* (*Eupatorium rugosum* 'Braunlaub'), the taller asters and *Helenium* all respond well to such treatment.

The hoops that make the staking so straightforward were hand-made from lengths of 5mm mild steel. Friends with a country garden had made up a plywood former, which made fast work of bending them in quantity. There are two sizes, one about knee height, the other waist height, which is ideal for the taller perennials. The rusted metal blends into the planting never to be seen again as soon as it is covered with foliage. Putting the stakes in takes minutes if you get to the plants while they are still low and can grow into their supports. Leave it too late and a pleasurable job becomes a fiddle, with all the anxiety of plants bundled and snapped and compromised in the process.

Wisteria

The wisteria was the first plant I put in the ground after moving in but, in the first three years of its life here, it withheld flowering, despite my best efforts at cultivation. I expect it would have flowered for me sooner had it been on a hot, south-facing wall instead of having first to rise up out of the well created by the extension. Those first years were a tease and a disappointment. In April, I watched the dark triangular buds vigilantly but they ran to leaf and not flower. I knew my grafted plant would not take the twenty-five years that a seed-raised specimen takes to flower, but I still felt the impatience.

I paid good money for my grafted Japanese *Wisteria floribunda* 'Alba', and when I carefully untangled the stems from the cane, there was already enough growth to make a modest impression by the window. I pruned exactly according to the rules and even fed it with tomato feed to encourage flowers. It just needed time to settle in. The fourth spring yielded the first seven racemes, the fifth there were double that number and, by the sixth, it was no longer possible to count.

The limbs are now the best part of four storeys high and would continue to ascend if I didn't prevent them from doing so. Growing over the west wall, it wraps onto the northern flank of the extension and jumps over the top, where those branches can bask in a blaze of heat. This is where it is happiest, and the limbs here present a completely different habit from those on the cooler walls. They have formed a mass of flowering spurs with little extension growth because they have no need to send out excess growth searching for light. The buds here swell two weeks ahead of the rest, and the unevenness of flowering across the plant caused by these different conditions is marvellous, as it extends the flowering season. It also gives you more than one chance to witness the miraculous transformation.

Juvenile flowers on the wisteria.

The wisteria is my equivalent of a blossom tree, and I love that it marks the transition from one season to the next with such exuberance. I have deliberately laced the branches around the windows so that you can witness from inside the buds swelling as the weather warms. The tough metallic sheaths break free to reveal the compacted racemes as soft as bees' bodies and just as furry. I check on progress daily when the sap is in the limbs. The anticipation of what is yet to come is the greater part of the pleasure, and I love the feeling of spring captured in the plant, the buds as big as the end of your thumb before they tilt away to expand and drop like streamers.

I prefer the Japanese species to the shorter-flowered Chinese *Wisteria sinensis* – the racemes are three times longer and taper from top to bottom in their most perfect moment. This, for me, is when the first few flowers open and the descending sequence of flower is yet to come below them. The moment lasts only a few days before the spell is broken and the walls are covered with a waterfall of flower.

I shall never forget one spring in Japan during the hanami (cherry blossom) festival. At twilight, an ancient cherry tree with a dark twist of limbs was lit by braziers carefully placed under its canopy. The flickering light picked out the first few blossoms, but there was the weight of expectancy in the buds. My wisteria marks the changing of the seasons here. By the time the racemes are white along their length, the lime-green foliage is sprung and the start of summer is with us.

Epimedium

I came upon my first *Epimedium* in the undergrowth of my childhood garden. It was a forgotten garden that had been overgrown for the best part of fifty years. For the most part, it had returned to woodland, and the seeding laurel, birch and bramble had established a new status quo. It would have been April, and the flush of nettles that had concealed it from view was already burgeoning, but the new leaves were unfurling regardless of the competition. The old foliage looked like beaten copper and was clattery to the touch, but the new leaves were what caught my attention. They were unbelievably soft and vulnerable-looking, heart-shaped and delicately veined with a wine-red dappling. Among them danced a myriad of what appeared to be tiny aquilegias of the palest primrose, and the winged flowers were suspended on cable-thin stems. It was love at first sight.

Epimedium pubescens.

The delicate appearance of *Epimedium* x *versicolor* 'Sulphureum' belies its hardiness, and the endurance of this original plant was testament to that. It had survived shade, drought, competition and neglect and, from the day of my first discovery, I have never gardened without them. Back then, over thirty years ago now, a small raft of European *Epimedium* was available on the market and, when I studied at Wisley, I soon learned that they were a mainstay of shade gardening. In recent years, and much to my delight, the Asiatic species from China and Japan have become available. If you were to read up about the Asian species, you might think that they were a delicate tribe, not up to the lifestyle of their swarthy cousins, but this has been far from the case here in the shady parts of my garden. It is true that they demand summer moisture, unlike their European cousins, which can hunker down in dry shade once established, but that can easily be arranged with the addition of garden compost and careful placing away from tree roots.

I have quickly developed a small obsession and now have about a dozen different species and several named forms tucked away into the cool corners. Obsessions are my way of getting to know a new field of plants. I have had them with magnolias, scented-leaved pelargoniums and species roses, to name but a few, but I am pleased to say that I have never been a train spotter in this regard. I do not have to have each and every one of a genus, but I like to run the experiment thoroughly and this involves selecting several favourites and finding a way to live with them for a few years. The best are those that prove themselves in terms of beauty and adaptability, while the ones that are either difficult, or not to my taste, fall by the wayside.

Epimedium are happy to live in the shade of other plants, as long as it is not all-eclipsing. The best shade is deciduous, and later emerging perennials easily provide it, while the *Epimedium* are seizing the early spring. The peony 'Late Windflower' is a good partner, as are many of the ferns. Where I have run out of space in the ground, I have taken to keeping the *Epimedium* in terracotta pans. These are brought up close to the house and kept on the shady windowsills in the spring, then returned to the holding ground down by the compost heap for the summer. It is cool there and I can keep an eye on the watering.

Epimedium 'Amanogawa'.

When they're up close and in pots, you can witness every stage of their delicate unfurlings. The Japanese hybrid 'Amanogawa' is first to stir, and the new foliage resembles unfurling fingers. The chocolate-coloured stems elongate beyond the canopy of last year's foliage and splay to the length of your hand and forearm combined. The flowers, which are held like a constellation and in their hundreds, are purest white. 'Amanogawa' means 'river of stars'. Reflexed to reveal a burnt orange keel, which fades to yellow at the tips, the flowers are without the spurs so characteristic of the genus, but they are exquisitely poised in the air like falling blossom. Although you can cut the oldest leaves back to the base as soon as you see the new growth emerging in March, I do not do this with plants that are still establishing because I believe they need all the energy they can muster. In a pot, it is easy to strip out the tired leaves as they fail and this is all that is necessary to keep them looking smart.

Epimedium membranaceum flowers for a good two months, starting in early April and, some years, continuing on into early June. The flowers are large, winged and golden yellow and held nicely above the newly emerging foliage, which is crazed bronze and green. *Epimedium davidii* is a yolkier yellow, and so far it has proven to be choosier here. This small-growing species was introduced from Sichuan in 1985. I first saw it growing in Beth Chatto's garden on the occasion that I was introduced to the plum-leaved *Polygonatum* x *hybridum* 'Betburg'. I have since combined them in the garden and like the warmth in the coupling very much. The gold of *E. davidii* is made that much more distinct because the foliage is a rich blood-red when emerging. I have had to move it around the garden three or four times to find a place that it likes, as it resents being overshadowed. The open shade of a north wall is perfect.

Foliage of *Epimedium membranaceum*.

The emerging foliage of the *Epimedium* is easily as delightful as the flowers. *Epimedium myrianthum* has long, evergreen leaves, which are a rich, shiny green when matured, but they go through an incredible transformation to get there. Filling out as they rise unformed above the old leaves, the new foliage inflates like a dragonfly expanding after emerging from the chrysalis. As it does so, the leaf is stained with a dark mottling, crazed like broken glass or smashed ice floating on water. It is my favourite plant in the garden while it is doing this, and embodies the fragility and wonder of spring perfectly. The flowers, of which there can be up to 350 to a stem (I have never counted but some train spotters have), are tiny and white, like a mist above the leaves.

Epimedium acuminatum 'Galaxy' is also good in the early stages, and it could be argued that the foliage is better than the horizontal splays of snowy flowers. It is a rich coppery red and darkens to a lively laurel-green. The foliage of *E. fargesii* 'Pink Constellation' is dark by comparison. A rich, inky green, the leaves are long and shaped like an arrowhead. They also have a jagged quality about them and look as if they might prick you if you were to touch them, though they don't. The starry flowers are violet-mauve with darker keels on the undersides.

Epimedium wushanense is the most dramatic of those that I grow here. It has long-fingered foliage of a rich olive-green, with a marvellous jade-green underside. The flowers, which appear on stems almost a metre long, are the largest of the *Epimedium* that I have, as wide as a two pence piece and appearing over two months if the slugs don't get to them first. If there is one problem you could pin to this group of *Epimedium*, it is their vulnerability when new shoots are emerging. The shaded crowns are the perfect home to slugs and snails and you have to remember to set down bait as soon as the new shoots start into growth. *Epimedium wushanense* is by far the most desired as slug food, and this is painful if you lose a new batch of spring growth. In my experience, the plant will take a little more sun, and a warm position gives it the resilience it needs to get through the spring massacre. *Epimedium wushanense* 'Caramel' is a more compact form, with neater growth and more slender leaves. For some reason, it is far less prone to the slugs, and the orange and tan flowers are out for a good six weeks, spanning the whole of spring and dancing into early June in a dappled corner.

Spring Flowers

There is a teetering point while the hornbeam is hung with catkins when time seems more precious than usual. These are precious moments, which have a dream-like quality and you know they are not designed to last. A couple of bright days will change everything, the catkins drop to the deck as the pleated leaves in the hornbeam unfold

Epimedium membranaceum.

Epimedium wushanense 'Caramel'.

PAGE 129
Epimedium fargesii 'Pink Constellation'.

PAGES 130–1
New foliage on *Cercis canadensis* 'Forest Pansy'.

PAGES 132–3
Stylophorum lasiocarpum and *Epimedium myrianthum*.

PAGES 134–5
The green of new foliage starts to make its presence known.

and I know then that there is no holding back. If I could, I would take this week or ten days off and just be here in the garden to draw breath and watch the long-awaited change. There is movement in every corner – buds swelling on the wisteria, ferns unravelling in the shade, clematis climbing the fence and bulbs pushing through. You have to watch keenly if you are not to miss anything.

The new growth on the *Paeonia mlokosewitschii* has already expanded and coloured green from the dusky plum of just the week before, and the buds are tight as marbles with the yellow of flower just visible. I got to know 'Molly-the-Witch' at Wisley, where it grew among the *Euphorbia characias* under the high canopy of oaks. They are the picture of spring, rising from nothing and flowering by the time the leaves have filled out on the trees. We were given three-year-old seedlings by Chris and Toby Marchant at Orchard Dene Nurseries, wholesale suppliers to the trade, and it took another three years for them to flower. But the flowers, if truth be told, are only part of the joy, and by the time they arrive, I already feel rewarded. The single primrose-yellow cups reveal a pale boss of stamens, and in a warm spell they are gone in a week. Despite its fragile appearance, this early peony is adaptable and happy to be plunged into the dappled shade of the plants around it for the remainder of the summer, as long as the soil is hearty and retentive.

The *Paeonia delavayi*, which is constantly threatening to overwhelm the vegetable beds, is a seedling of a plant at the Edinburgh Botanic Garden. I was there for a year when I was nineteen, and I singled it out as something special and took a handful of the seedlings we were removing from its base while weeding. I had already fallen for the tree peonies some years earlier after growing a silken-flowered Japanese hybrid. The young growth is remarkable, emerging like a plum-coloured sea anemone from a gnarled bud the size of a horse chestnut. The stems are gaunt and naked at this point, and the buds swell fast, held in a cluster of calyx and leaves yet to come. The buds are like a crown, with their stems lengthening towards flowering and the leaves filling out around them like waving tentacles. The petals, held tightly around a boss of golden stamens, are smaller and darker than others of the species and the deepest red you can imagine, as dark as dried blood and satiny as an Elizabethan damask. I have underplanted them with *Milium effusum* 'Aureum' and *Dicentra spectabilis* 'Gold Heart', both of which have a complementary lightness in the leaf.

The *Allium* are now racing skyward. I have *A. hollandicum* 'Purple Sensation' on the shady side of the garden, where the dead nettle *Lamium orvala* are already hooded with sinister, hooded flowers. They

A posy of *Narcissus jonquilla* and *N.* 'Hawera', *Viola labradorica* (*Viola riviniana* Purpurea Group), *Pulmonaria saccharata* 'Leopard' and *Dicentra* 'Langtrees'.

Paeonia mlokosewitschii.

PAGE 136
Paeonia delavayi.

are a dark fleshy pink. This is a beefy plant when it gets going, sending roots deep down to find moisture, and happy in dry shade once it is away. The meaty red emerging foliage of *Paeonia* 'Late Windflower' nearby is a fine companion. The buds are unbelievably elegant and taper to a lone bone-white flower, which is the epitome of elegance.

At the end of the garden, I have *Allium stipitatum* 'Mount Everest', which comes at the end of the month with the *Aquilegia chrysantha* 'Yellow Star' and the last of the tree peonies. I enjoy the tapering conurbation of tiny Turkish domes while I wait for the *Allium* to open, and they rise daily with the gathering weight of foliage around them.

Anemone nemorosa 'Robinsoniana'.

The end of the garden, in the shadier parts, is where I have the greater majority of early treasures. These are constantly under threat from the *Stylophorum lasiocarpum*, which self-seeds freely now that it is happy. It is a modest-looking plant of considerable poise and has outstripped the *Meconopsis cambrica* in terms of vigour. Both have papery golden flowers and, at a distance, the two could be confused. On closer inspection, the Welsh poppy is quite a violent, acid yellow compared to the softer eggy yellow of the Chinese celandine poppy. I love both yellows for the way they light up the shadows.

The *Stylophorum* goes on to produce remarkable seed heads as the flowers go over later in May. They are tapered, covered in silver hairs and held perfectly upright, like candle flames in a still room. The Welsh poppy is a slower plant in all respects and flowers for longer. It is also happier to slip in among the other woodlanders without having to divide and conquer.

Trillium chloropetalum and a new shoot of D*isporum cantoniense* 'Night Heron'.

The *Trillium* have not been easy to grow here. They dwindle in the summer because the air gets too hot and dry for them, but I have mulched the shady areas at the end of the garden to build up the fertility and I now know that things are working. I have a fine form of *Trillium chloropetalum*, which rises up to knee height. The luxuriant ruff of foliage is chequered and slashed with red and cool grey-green, which makes a fine combination with the *Disporum cantoniense*. I have a dark-leaved form called 'Night Heron', and it is beautifully named, the long limbs rising up above their neighbours before arching over. They are as fine as asparagus in the first month after breaking ground, and you begin to wonder if anything could be more beautiful as the sheen of dark foliage expands in a delicate canopy over the green flowers that hang in their shade. This is not a difficult plant and, though it has taken three years or so to get to this size, it is certainly a 'doer'. I also have 'Green Giant', which I saw at Dan Hinkley's garden in Seattle. It had all the vigour of bamboo over in Seattle, but we shall see how it fares here.

The *Arisaema sikokianum* have lasted in the ground for a good three years, but they always decline in the winter wet now that the soil is rich and retentive. I have taken to keeping them in pots for the terrace and store them in the cold frame over winter. *Arisaeama* aside, soil fertility is everything. The constant improvement now means that the leafy *Paris quadrifolia*, which are planted among the *Dryopteris wallichiana*, are running freely, and the *Anemone nemorosa* are beginning to do the same. The pure white, double-flowered *Anemone nemorosa* 'Plenifolia' is a complete treasure and proving to be the slowest to spread, while the lilac-flowered 'Robinsoniana' is the most vigorous among the unfurling hart's-tongue ferns. They are happy because their fleshy rhizomes can run in the top layers of soil that are now friable with leaf mould.

Paris quadrifolia.

The early-flowering *Dicentra* 'Langtrees' is planted close to the path and I have to watch it if it is not to overwhelm the *Erythronium*. The dog's-tooth violets have been fickle here. They are some of my favourite spring flowers, with their marbled foliage and reflexed flowers held high above the leaf. Although they were happy in the mossy turf of my parent's garden, *E. dens-canis* has failed here on more than one occasion. However, *E.* 'Pagoda' is thriving in the sunshine with the *Pulmonaria*, and I have finally found a place that *E. californicum* 'White Beauty' favours. Sometimes you just have to keep on moving a plant around until you find a spot it likes, and the best time to move them is in-the-green, as soon as they have flowered. The secret of my ultimate success with 'White Beauty', after such a reticent start, seems to be that the *Dicentra* gently shades them, providing a little microclimate while they are at their most vulnerable. The *Dicentra* produces a six-week succession of pale teardrop flowers over finely dissected glaucous foliage before withering away to almost nothing, but the willow gentian, *Gentiana asclepiadea*, covers for it later. I always forget about it until it breaks, choking, through the *Dicentra* foliage, desperate by this time for light.

Erythronium 'Pagoda'.

The *Podophyllum hexandrum* moves fast once it breaks ground, the solitary leaves like the wings of a bat unfurling as they push through the soil and expand. The clump is now hearty and the marbled leaves are some of the finest. The lonely pale pink flowers held above the leaves are as delicate as quince blossom and last just a matter of days before starting to form their heavy fruits. Within a month, the *Podophyllum* is leafy and luxuriant, and most of the early performers are eclipsed by the *Veratrum* and the ferns as they fill out and provide cover. This leafy cover is important in terms of keeping things cool, but I always have to remember to mark the *Paris polyphylla* with a cane, as they don't emerge until May and always frighten me into thinking I have lost them. I also have a strict rule with myself that there will be no rootling around to check on their progress – one year, I broke a precious shoot in my impatience. The green crowns of flower last for what seems to be months.

Out in the sun and stealing time while the wave of summer perennials is mustering is the first and most spectacular umbellifer. *Molopospermum peloponnesiacum* is slow to get away, and the Molly-the-Witch are usually in bud before the ruff of foliage erupts close by. At first, the cluster of growth is a dark coppery red, but it rapidly fills out in a glorious awakening, stretching its limbs to form a glistening mound of finely cut foliage as beautiful as any fennel. They have taken about three years to build the strength to flower and they put everything into it. While the *Ferula tingitana* 'Cedric Morris' bolt and usually kill themselves in expending the energy to flower, the *Molopospermum* are completely perennial. One day, when I have the room, I will have a group of them large enough to walk among and interlace them with *Gladiolus tristis*. The wiry stems of this early gladiolus capture every breath of wind but it needs a sheltered spot so that its winter foliage does not get damaged. If I found the position where one could complement the other and do it en masse, I would be very happy indeed.

Molopospermum peloponnesiacum.

Foliage

In a matter of days, like a light going on, the garden is green once again. The electric green of the box pushes away from the darkness of the old growth and, for a week before it dims, it is as if lit from within. You can almost hear the sap rising as foliage sweeps the boundaries, the ground plane and walls where there are climbers. Houses that have been visible since November are suddenly gone behind the sycamores, which shake themselves into life in a flurry.

Gladiolus tristis.

Foliage is one of the most important elements in a garden, and I am happy for it to be the predominant force and the foundation to the planting. I rely upon it for texture, be it shiny and smooth or puckered and light-absorbing, and I use it for form and movement. Positioned carefully, to underpin the colour of flower, it can engender a range of differing moods to give each area of the garden its own particular atmosphere, whether lush, dry, Asian, Mediterranean or closer to home. The simple, unassuming green of the hornbeam allows me to play with a range of differing 'stories' in its orbit, while the scale and rich green of the fig near the vegetable beds hold your eye and make you aware of the productive nature of this area. Small leaves are far less attention-seeking than large, demanding foliage.

The giant dinner-plate-sized leaves of the *Vitis coignetiae* go through an extraordinary transformation in these days between seasons. Clasped tight like a tiny fist, they are silvery pink as they emerge. The mature leaves are puckered, matte and light-absorbing. By the time the *Tetrapanax* has expanded, it is the biggest of all the leaves in the garden, but they start small, rising up and away from the crown on an ever-lengthening petiole. In a rainstorm, you can shelter under a leaf, but if it hails in June (and it so often does), the leaves can be completely lacerated. I have the hardiest form of *Tetrapanax papyrifer* named 'Rex', which came from Great Dixter. The young foliage is ginger and overlaid with a powdery indumentum. Some people find this an irritant. Indeed, it catches in my throat when I am working among it, but that is the worst of it for me, and I value the cooling aesthetic of the leaves.

Tetrapanax papyrifer 'Rex'.

'Rex' used to be in the front garden, but I moved them to the back because I felt they were attracting too much attention, and it is important for me that the front garden is quiet and unassuming – to a point. Each cane lasts about four years before failing. However, they run quite freely and come up usually where you don't want them – in their original position, they got beneath a wall and came up in the neighbour's front garden. If you want to increase the plant, you can promote suckering by hoeing among the roots, but you need only so many in a garden this size, as the scale of the foliage draws your eye to them immediately.

Look closely and you will see that there are a thousand different greens and that no two are identical. The *Euphorbia mellifera* is an emerald-, light-filled green, while holly and ivy are dark enough to act like shadows. I have let the ivy run over the fences at the end of the garden to create an illusion of more depth, and each year we have the tiny holly blue butterflies, which use it as a breeding ground.

Melianthus major.

The light-reflecting silvers literally throw light back at you and they act as wayfinders in moonlight. I still miss the *Salix exigua*, which lived fast and died young after six or seven years, but its long, narrow foliage was like a shoal of tiny fish when it was in its prime. There was always movement in the branches and it was an adaptable foil to whatever found itself in the area. Grey foliage tends to look most comfortable in the sun and makes you think of dry, free-draining places, which is why I like the *Melianthus major* up by the terrace. This is one of the few plants that I kept from the roof garden in Vauxhall, and I love the sharply serrated edge to the leaf, which looks as though it has been cut with pinking shears. It could do with more sun where it is, planted in the lee of the *Euphorbia mellifera*. As the garden grows, the habitat here is being gently dominated by shade and, consequently, the grey-greens are beginning to look out of place. In the main, I keep them over on the sunny side.

Astelia chathamica is a rare exception because it is more than happy in shade and is valuable for bringing light to dark corners. I used to have three at the shady end, but they began to feel too dominant with their long, spear-like growth and exotic feel. I prefer the garden softer these days, and most of the the architectural plants have been replaced by gentler foliage. The *Galanthus* have blue-green foliage, which also throws light into spring shade, and I like the leaf almost as much as the flower for the foil it provides for the newly emerging coppery *Actaea* (formally known as *Cimicifuga*). I team them up with *Pulmonaria saccharata* 'Leopard', which this early on is scattered with bi-coloured flowers and covered with bees. Later in the summer, when the foliage fills out, the leaves are spotted with silver (hence the name) and light up the ground in the shade beneath the *Tetrapanax*.

Pulmonaria saccharata 'Leopard'.

The young foliage of the *Actaea racemosa* is brown when young, but it expands rapidly to green. Several plants have a similar bronzing when young: the *Rodgersia* 'Herkules', the *Ageratina altissima* (*Eupatorium rugosum* 'Braunlaub') and, most striking of all, the *Rosa* x *odorata* 'Mutabilis'. 'Mutabilis' is almost at its best just before it flowers and the foliage is a coppery, chocolate-brown.

Golden foliage is as life-giving as sunlight and, if it's positioned carefully, it can fool you into thinking the sun is out when it isn't. I use it sparingly because it can flare out in the open, but in shade I like it immensely. The shade-loving *Milium effusum* 'Aureum' helps to keep the dark *Paeonia delavayi* from being too sombre. I have grown this unassuming grass since I was a child, and I like the way it seeds about without ever dominating. I grow it between *Iris chrysographes*, so that the blackened flowers rise up into the pale inflorescence of the grass, and it also helps to make the *Hemerocallis lilioasphodelus* sparkle. *Dicentra spectabilis* 'Gold Heart' is surprisingly effective, despite the fact that I'm really not sure that the leaves go at all well with the candy-pink of the flower. Hopefully, one of these days, someone will find a white-flowered form, but until then I will keep it in the shadows. The biennial *Smyrnium perfoliatum*, which is dangerous if it likes you and self-seeds, is as acid green as the 'Gold Heart' is golden, but I risk using it under the *Rosa* 'Cooperi' for the injection of light it provides early in the summer.

Foliage of *Rosa* x *odorata* 'Mutabilis'.

With the exception of the *Pulmonaria* and the marbled leaves of the *Epimedium* and the *Podophyllum*, I avoid variegation because I find it confuses the eye. If I need something bright, or striking, I take the purist's route and keep things simple. It allows far greater freedom when you come to consider the overlay of flower.

I would grow more ferns if there were room – I never tire of their foliage, which is restful, cooling and undemanding. As a group, ferns are hugely adaptable. The *Dryopteris setiferum*, with its lacy, horizontal growth, is proof of this, surviving in the root-infested ground under the hornbeam along with *Cyclamen coum*. The huddle of hart's-tongues, given to us by a friend from Cornwall, lines the path up to the compost heap, and their shiny year-round foliage bounces light around in the shade. I am happy to see that they do well here, and I think that the limy rubble in the ground at the foot of the wall must have made them feel at home. The unfurling fronds are silver-white and, as they start to unroll, I cut away the old foliage to make way for the spill of the new leaf.

Dryopteris wallichiana is by far the most dramatic of the ferns. The knuckles are covered with thick, bronze hair before they unfurl, which gives them the appearance of bears' paws. Once they have unfurled, the crosiers are black and lime. The old leaves will have kept going almost to the end of winter, and I leave them as long as I can before reducing them back to the knuckle at ground level. It has taken time to build up the soil fertility for them to do well here, but they reach almost a metre in height before the cones open out and relax. The prehistoric-looking *Blechnum chilense* has never done as well as it might here, despite my best attempts. Some plants can be perplexing. I had read about this fern liking damp, moisture-retentive ground, but my parents grow it beautifully in sandy shade. No amount of compost seems to make it happy here and, as it is a fern that only looks good when it is thriving, I have finally acknowledged that I must find it a new home.

At the base of the *Drypoteris* I am starting to have success with *Adiantum venustum*. This hardy maidenhair fern creeps slowly through friable leaf mould when it is happy. The wire-thin stems are pitch-black and the foliage pale and shimmering. I would grow it in all the dark places if I could. You can play with delicate foliage as much as you can with the drama of a larger leaf. Working on a small scale allows you to draw the eye in to the detail. If you look down into the *Adiantum*, you see nearby the shiny simplicity of *Asarum europaeum* as a counterpoint, the arching dusky growth of *Polygonatum* x *hybridum* 'Betburg', with foliage that is plum-purple when young,

Dryopteris wallichiana emerging through *Asarum europaeum* and *Adiantum venustum*.

Polygonatum x *hybridum* 'Betberg'.

and the bright, cut leaves of *Meconopsis cambrica*. The fronding blue-green leaf of *Dicentra* 'Langtrees' moves the greens towards the ethereal silvery-grey of *Athyrium* 'Ghost', a deciduous fern that is thriving here. The textures work so well together that I often wonder if flowers are superfluous.

Vegetables

My mother grew vegetables and her father before her. She was brought up in vicarages during wartime and had picked up the phrase, 'And it's all from the garden!' to accompany a summer-time meal. I now know the joy in that phrase and, in the last few years, have returned to growing vegetables with commitment. I got out of the habit while I was without my own land, but growing my greens has become an increasingly important part of life here in the city. We know where our food has come from and that it has been produced with love. It is organic and we can enjoy it while it is still pulsing with life, freshly picked and vital.

The two raised beds at the end were devoted to vegetables until I took on the allotment. Today, the brighter of the two has been given over to herbs. There are three types of mint: black peppermint for tea, and apple and garden mint for cooking, plunged in plastic pots to keep them within bounds. Next to them are sorrel and chives. You don't need many plants of either. In the hottest part, there are rows of thyme, oregano and sage, all of which hate to be overshadowed. In recent years, the fat, metallic rosemary beetle has started to plague the sage and the rosemary regularly. This newcomer to London is a potential threat to the sage family, but otherwise the herbs are easy, as long as you remember to pick off the beetles and dispose of them with haste.

The herbs that we require in quantity, such as coriander, dill and parsley, are grown in rows on the allotment. When the frame is emptied for the summer, I plant up several pans with different varieties of basil, as they are only reliable in this country when given heat. I vary them every year, but would not want to be without the spicy Violetto Aromatico and Classico Italiano, which still makes the best pesto. Lemon verbena, for tea, and pineapple sage (also a victim to the rosemary beetle) are grown in pots. Both are delicious to rub between finger and thumb when passing, and they are kept in prominent places in sunshine for exactly this purpose.

The cooler of the two beds is ideal for leafy salad vegetables, which we use daily throughout the summer. The beds, which are constructed

Athyrium 'Ghost'.

First salad seedlings.

PAGE 145
Box mounds are a structural foil for the new foliage of *Molinia caerulea* subsp. *arundinacea* 'Transparent'.

PAGES 146–7
Wisteria floribunda 'Alba' on the back of the house.

PAGES 148–9
Cloches protect the new salad crops.

PAGES 150–1
Paeonia 'Late Windflower' growing with *Valeriana officinalis* and *Allium hollandicum* 'Purple Sensation'.

from roofing joists, are raised, as much as a means of demarcation as to make them easy to tend. It is incredible what we get out of them if the space is planned carefully. Sowing in succession is the secret, and we have a three-weekly sowing rota to keep us in salad throughout the summer. If the weather is warm, wild rocket and an Italian leafy mix of chicories, dandelion and lettuce are sown in late March. I break the rules and broadcast an area as wide as the cloche. However, you need to sow as thinly as you can to prevent overcrowding, and the first few batches are brought along with the warmth of the protective cloche. Mustard greens are fast and hardy and can do without the protection as soon as the soil warms to 6ºC. You have to be vigilant and thin regularly if you are not to create a hiding place for slugs and snails, and I harvest the thinnings until the spacing is right to let the plants go. Certain lettuces, such as 'Little Gem', and the mizuna heart up better when grown in a more orderly fashion. On the allotment, I keep to rows where order is needed to save time on weeding and thinning.

I originally grew the tomatoes on tripods against the sunny fence. Here they had the benefit of the extra heat and I loved how they looked, coloured up and bright alongside the dahlias. But, one damp summer, they succumbed to blight and since then I have been rotating them from place to place on the allotment. This extra piece of ground always feels like the straw that will break the camel's back in a busy spring and, despite its proximity, I have to make myself go there to get the work done. You can build up a sweat on a good day's digging and I miss that now that the gardening I do here is all about the detail. A hard day's dig is good for the soul but, once the potatoes are in, the majority of the hard work is done. The allotment can be easily maintained on about two hours per week, which is nothing if you get the timing right.

We grow enough vegetables in this piece of borrowed ground to keep us from having to buy any throughout the summer. Kale and broccoli start the season in February, and early, blight-resistant spuds such as 'Lady Christl' are an absolute treat. Eight rows are just enough not to tire of them, and eating seasonally is all part of the pleasure. There are oak and cos lettuces grown in rows to heart up, and perpetual spinach and mustard greens, which bolt at the first sign of drought. There is only a water butt on the allotment and I have to ration water, which is a good exercise in getting to know which plants you can get away with growing.

I don't grow dwarf French beans because climbing beans are easier to pick, or runners because it's nice to have varieties that are hard to buy in the market. Four tripods of deluxe black bamboo (harvested

PAGE 152
Rosa banksiae 'Lutea'.

from the hedge in the garden), are sown sequentially with green and yellow flat-podded beans and borlotti beans. These Italian beans from Seeds of Italy are quite the most delicious and we eat them by the bowlful with butter and sea salt. The purple podded beans, Cosse Violette, look great, but they turn green when boiled, so we pick them while they are still tiny and add them as a colourful and crunchy addition to salads. Picking young is one of the great joys of growing your own vegetables. The three courgette plants have to be watched very carefully if we are not to end up with a host of marrows. I grow yellow and green bush varieties and also enjoy the flowers deep-fried.

The two rows of dahlias and sunflowers on the allotment, which would now take up too much room in the garden, are for cutting, as are the sweet peas, which grow up the chain-link fence surrounding the plot. In the shade of the hedge, there is a patch of 'Autumn Bliss' raspberries, which were salvaged from the previous owner when we took over the allotment. One day, when I have more ground, I will expand upon this essential aspect of the year's gardening but, for now, this rectangle of borrowed land helps in keeping things grounded.

Roses

If I had more space, and I realize while putting my ruminations into words that it must be something that I think about with increasing regularity, I would love to have a cutting garden. It would be set aside in an area all its own, which would include the more mundane things, such as the compost heaps, a greenhouse, cold frames and the vegetables. The beds would be workmanlike, the roses set out in rows like vegetables, so that they would be easy to look after and to gather. I would grow them in abundance, so that we could pick without inhibition. Contained in this way, it wouldn't matter if they bore no relation to the garden beyond the boundaries. As misfits, it would be fine if they were gangly or awkward from the neck down, or that their colours were not particularly 'tasteful' for a garden setting. All these things would be forgiven for their productivity and the fact that they sat well in a jug.

Certain for inclusion – as individuals they are far from perfect – would be a selection of roses. I would grow 'Fantin-Latour', 'Madame Hardy' and 'Tuscany Superb' for their quartered blooms, and I would not have to worry that they only bloomed once. I would have 'Louis XIV' and be able to ignore the blackspot, as one velvety flower in a bud vase would be all that I needed. There would be roses selected for scent at the expense of bad behaviour elsewhere, or if included in the garden, would drive things in the wrong direction because of their opulence.

That said, I would miss having roses in the garden and their inclusion has been made that much easier having made the decision not to use any that feel too far removed from their natural state. I want to garden with roses in a naturalistic way here, to retain their character as shrubs and to be able to rely upon their structure and foliage as much as I do their fleeting flowers. Health, vigour and grace come top of the list of preferred attributes, and I have avoided the problems that come from overbreeding because the roses I have selected are just one step away from their parent. The fact that their flowers are small or with just a hint of perfume is the compromise.

Whittling down my favourites has not been easy. I have done without *Rosa glauca* because the distinctive silvery foliage would be wrong among the greens. I also miss out on the crimson dog roses and the flaming hips of *Rosa moyesii* because there simply isn't space. There are many others as well, far too many to mention, as I do not have the trees into which I can send favourite ramblers, or the meadows into which I can let the larger shrub roses loose. Although roses are, in the main, long-lived and can survive generations when happy, there have been failures here, too. I had to part with the incense rose, *Rosa primula*, after it struggled here for five or six years. This early, once-flowering rose is one of the first to bloom in April, with tiny buds opening to primrose-yellow dog roses. They come with spring blossom and the first flush of fresh new growth. Though their flowers are transitory, the plant is distinctive for its ferny foliage. This is sticky with essential oils that emit a musky smell on damp mornings or after a spring shower, which is redolent of Catholic churches. This delicious scent was why I grew it, but this is a rose that needs light and air around it to do well and, after struggling for a while, the honey fungus that still rattles around the garden finally did for it.

The roses here have to be the survivors. 'Mermaid' is the oldest plant in the garden and survived the cull after we moved here because it is a rose that is hard not to love. Despite its rangy habit, it is a climber that doesn't like to be directed, with angular limbs that snap if you try to do so. There is charm in this unwieldiness. It grows on the north-facing fence, not an ideal position for any rose, and has rushed up to the top where the light is. I prune it to a framework in February, which keeps it in line with the top of the fence, but over the summer it sends out thorn-clad arching stems on wood that darkens almost to black. The foliage is shiny apple-green, though in a dry spring it needs

Scented foliage of *Rosa primula*.

spraying early on if it is not to succumb to mildew. The first of the flowers emerge from long, pointed buds clad in a tapering calyx, and they open wide, to the width of a small hand, the soft yellow single petals twisted and uneven around a spectacular boss of golden stamens. The scent is light but pleasant, if you dare to get close enough among the thorns.

Yellow is a good colour to open the year, and the *Rosa banksiae* 'Lutea' planted on the east-facing front of the house is often out around my birthday in the second week of April. I fell in love with its cousin, the cream-flowered 'Alba-Plena', one Easter in Rome. It was cascading from a garden over the length of a high wall in Trastevere and filling the streets with the scent of violets. It took a couple of years for my plant on the front of the house to flower, time enough for it to run up over the porch. Only then did it become clear that the nurserymen who supplied it had labelled it incorrectly as 'Lutea'. Although 'Lutea' has just the tiniest hint of perfume, more the smell of ozone than a perfume, it is delightful and in many ways I am pleased for the mistake. 'Alba-Plena' is shy to flower in Britain because its wood needs more heat than a British summer can provide to ripen it enough to produce flowers. Although the heat on the wall at the front is gone by midday, London living is enough to compensate and 'Lutea' is festooned when in season.

Rosa banksiae 'Lutea'.

The very first buds are already formed in early March and they emerge with new green foliage among the evergreen leaves of the previous year. Their arrival precipitates a change of foliage, the oldest leaves dropping as the new arrive but, by the end of March, the arching growth is fresh and covered with potential. A wonderful couple of weeks follow as the promise of the flower begins to show itself, one bud unfurling here to be followed by another and another until the whole plant is covered. There is a perfect moment somewhere in the month of flowering when there are as many buds as open flowers, potential and reward at the same time. People on the street comment on it, and it is a joy to go in and out of the house. If I let it, it would be up to the top of the four storeys so, during the summer and after it has produced a new set of branches, I remove the majority of the longest wands, leaving a few to take the place of the oldest limbs. Though it can be pruned back to a framework close to the support at this stage, I think it takes the grace from the plant, as the joy is in the spill of limbs.

Rosa 'Cooperi'.

The *Rosa* 'Cooperi', also known as Cooper's Burmese, is evergreen, too, though with large and lustrous apple-green foliage. The plant covers what must now be the remains of a trelliswork extension that sits on top of the wall at the end of the garden. One of these days I am going to have to reduce it back to a framework in winter but, to date, I have reduced just the longest limbs with a pair of long-armed loppers. This is not ideal, but the rose is a brute and you only have to reach for your secateurs and it has you in a lethal grip. Consequently, it makes a perfect burglar-proof barrier, but it would be a mistake to put it on a boundary where the neighbours were not likeminded.

I love this rose for its simplicity. Its single ivory-white flowers, like oversized dog roses, pop from tapering buds and open one at a time along the arching stems. The display starts in early May in tandem with the white *Allium* and the *Aquilegia chrysantha* 'Yellow Star' and continues for the best part of five weeks, the flowers flecked with a dirty grey-pink just before they drop. This is all part of their appeal, and I bring them into the house to witness the buds opening and the boss of stamens darkening as the flowers age. For a single-flowered rose, they last a surprisingly long time and, if I leave the limbs in the jar, they will root in a fortnight or so, ready for potting up. I was given this rose as a cutting and, as they are so easy to take, I play to this lust for life and always pot up a few to keep in the frame and give away as gifts.

Rosa x *odorata* 'Mutabilis' and *Rosa* x *odorata* 'Bengal Crimson' are the only recurrent roses in the garden. I would not want to be without either. Both need a warm position to do well, and you can tell just by looking at them that they are related. Twiggy growth that branches and rebranches continually throughout the growing season forms large and impossible-to-prune shrubs, two to three metres in height and as much across when weighed down with rain. Regular deadheading is all they need to keep them in good condition, but I have resorted to drastic action every five years or so to keep the bushes from toppling. By reducing them to a main framework before growth starts in very early spring, you can encourage a new framework but, be warned, they take a good year to come back and look the part again.

Although both can be in flower at Easter, 'Bengal Crimson' is usually the first and it has even given me flowers at Christmas. The winter flowers are a washed-out pink, but those that come with the warmth of the new season are sumptuous. The numerous buds are long, tapering and pointed, held in loose clusters. They throw themselves open and fade, the blood drained out of them in a day. I love this dishevelled flower with one petal always crumpled, and the flower never flat. It is also without perfume, but I will always find it a home where there's a warm corner.

'Mutabilis' leafs up early, coppery new foliage replacing the leaves that hang on during winter. This is as much part of the joy of spring as the first flowers, and I will (begrudgingly) spray just once at this

Rosa x *odorata* 'Mutabilis'.

Rosa x *odorata* 'Bengal Crimson'.

point for mildew and blackspot because they can be susceptible. Again, the flowers appear in many-headed clusters and they open and last just three days. At first, they are apricot but, in time, and as the name implies, they change – to cerise and, finally, to a dark carmine. The effect is as if the bush is covered in thousands of butterflies, their wings opening and closing.

Potting-On

As the bulbs go over, they are moved to a holding corner in the sunshine because they need at least five to six weeks for the foliage to regenerate the bulb. Herein lies an awkward handover, as there are new plants waiting for the pots to be vacated. I wait as long as I can, usually until the first fortnight in May, before decanting the bulbs into trays. They are shaken free of soil and dried off like onions in the sun on the terrace before going into the garage for the summer. The soil is reconditioned with new compost from the heap and some blood, fish and bone, in preparation for the annuals. I use my own garden soil taken from the vegetable beds as the base for the potting compost since it is now light and friable after years of improvement. I rotate it every other year, to make sure that it is not depleted by intensive growing.

Periods of flux are to be expected, and the end of the garden starts to look like a nursery garden, with the hardiest of the half-hardy annuals already in the frame and the more tender waiting for the first shift to be moved under the cover of a cloche.

Acclimatizing your plants is time well spent for they have to make some adjustment before they are tough enough to be happy out in the open. By the beginning of May, I am keen for everything to be off the windowsills and for the garage to be liberated.

Although the frame offers light protection in the winter and a warmer environment in the growing season, the garage is completely frost-free. Sandwiched between the tall walls of our house and the neighbour's, a clear corrugated plastic roof makes it light enough to hold the tender perennials while they are in a state of semi-dormancy. The *Pelargonium* and the *Brugmansia* have been kept just moist over the winter but, now the light levels are up, they are straining to get out. The plants are lifted into the sunshine and stripped of dead foliage, then repotted into improved compost. They are held in the shelter of the terrace for a fortnight until being taken down the garden. The *Cosmos atrosanguineus* and begonias are turned out and repotted, but it is important not to overwater them at this stage, even if the sun is out.

They need just enough to get them started because the nights are still cold, and cold and wet in combination are lethal.

I have started using mycorrhizal fungi with all the new planting, as the *Nicotiana suaveolens* in particular have been plagued by verticillium wilt. The *Nicotiana* have modest root systems and can easily sit in compost that lies wet if I don't use the shallow pans. I sprinkle the fungi, which are in granulated form, in the bottom of the planting hole, and they start working within a fortnight to three weeks. They form a symbiotic relationship once they have bonded with the plant's roots and assist with nutrient uptake and drought resistance. I use them now as a matter of course and feel that it is definitely making a difference with new plantings, which seem heartier.

When the weather is reliably warm and the plants are toughened up, the *Cleome* and *Nicotiana sylvestris* are shoehorned into what have now become tiny gaps between the perennials. I use them for their late summer colour, but they have to be watched for a month or so, otherwise the slugs will get them when they are new, fresh and tasty. Weeks of care can be obliterated overnight if you do not exercise control. Organic slug pellets need to be reapplied weekly if it is raining, and I keep vigil after showers. The snails that come out after the rain are picked over and hurled into my neighbour's garden. I hear that snails have a homing instinct but I hope they will be satisfied by the nettles and brambles next door and will decide to set up home there.

Bamboo

The bamboo hedge that runs along the terrace provides the illusion of privacy and makes a valuable contribution to the feeling of oasis. When you are standing underneath the hedge, the lofty house next door is completely concealed from view and we are often surprised when eating out on summer evenings to hear our neighbours' voices just feet away. On all but the stillest of days, there is movement in the branches, and the rustle of foliage is a baffle to the hubbub of London. When there is wind, you can see the airflow coursing through the length of the hedge like a ripple on water, and when it rains, the canes arch to touch the ground. I love how they harness the elements in this way, and even after they have been weighed almost horizontal by snow, they bounce back oblivious.

The weight of green is never heavy because the hedge is always shifting in the breeze, and the simplicity of the single line sits well with the emptiness of the terrace. The shadow patterns on the clean

New shoots of *Phyllostachys nigra*.

uninterrupted stone are hypnotic. Bamboo is undeniably exotic and you have to be careful where you use it, as it can very easily look at odds with the wrong palette of plants, but close to buildings and in an urban setting, it is perfect. The bamboo likes the shelter that the buildings afford it here and, with water and good living, it has grown almost to the bedroom windows.

As the weather warms in May, the new shoots break the leaf litter that catches among the stems of previous years. The spears are squat and expectant, and as soon as they get going, they push through aggressively with all the force of the plant's massive root system behind them. Their ascendancy is something that you have to be part of, and over the next month I check on them daily. On warm days after rain, they grow more than a centimetre an hour, and in no time the new culms are up among the canopy, making their way to the light. They have reached their ultimate height here now, but there are usually one or two that top the rest or appear to until they fill out and arch over. They must be at least seven metres high now.

I feed the plants in April with blood, fish and bone and, when they are in growth, I soak them weekly because the expenditure of this amount of energy is depleting. This is the only time that I consider the bamboos to be messy – as they put on new leafage on the oldest canes in June and July, they drop a flurry of old foliage. You can tell that the new canes have reached their ultimate height and have started to branch when the papery sheaths covering the culms break free and come clattering to earth.

The fresh canes of *Phyllostachys nigra* are blue-green and take a year to blacken. It takes five or seven years until they turn grey and, finally, fade to white, when they die. They rarely get to this point here because, late in July or some time in August, I prune out the oldest and the weakest canes so that there is space between the uprights. The wood soon blunts the loppers, which I push deep into the leaf litter so that the cuts are as low as possible. It is also imperative to make a straight cut across the grain of the culm because a diagonal cut will leave an extremely dangerous spike. After the canes are reduced back to the best and the most upright, the lowest side branches are also removed so that we can get the benefit of the blackened wood without interruption. This makes a huge difference to the feeling of airiness, and we can sit neatly under the canopy on the stone bench at their base. The canes that are removed are trimmed back and used for staking on the allotment.

Phyllostachys nigra is supposedly a clump-forming bamboo and should be safe in this narrow slot of a bed that separates us from our

Phyllostachys nigra.

PAGE 161
Potting on pelargoniums and other tender perennials.

PAGES 162–3
The upper terrace makes an event of early summer rains.

PAGES 164–5
Rosa x odorata 'Mutabilis'.

PAGES 166–7
Early summer from the deck.

neighbours. The original plants were bought in two batches and I am convinced that I have two forms, as one of them has begun to creep. I had four large plants originally and divided them with an old saw to make the eight that form the hedge and, though you cannot tell from the top growth, the roots are beginning to signify something else. Only a couple of canes have escaped under the fence but I wouldn't plant them again in such close proximity to neighbours without putting in a serious root barrier. My neighbours, I might add, have enjoyed the bamboo, too, and it takes no time to retain the trespassing stems when they are soft and fresh and newly visible. Not all *Phyllostachys* are as accommodating. The *Phyllostachys viridiglaucescens* at the end is a runner and I have to cut these runners back every summer to stop it advancing from the clump. If I were to start again, I would have contained the plant within a double row of overlapping concrete slabs. Buried on their sides and overlapped, they would keep the brute at bay.

Phyllostachys are far less prone to flowering than many other bamboos. Flowering has a devastating effect, defoliating adult plants in a season. Stressful conditions or a dry summer will often cause it. The best thing to do if it happens is dig them out and start with a different genus.

Iris

Several irises have already worked their way through the garden over the years, but even they are just a handful of what is available in the trade. The bearded iris has never been included because they feel too opulent for the company they would be keeping here. I grew them among old-fashioned roses at Home Farm, using dark, inky blue varieties with dusky Oriental poppies. I have also planted them en masse in myriad colours in Italy for the spectacle they bring to a garden in early summer. But, in the cool of the garden here, I am happy to keep to the smaller-flowering forms and seek them out rather than be drawn to them like beacons.

What has influenced my choice is as much to do with the growing conditions as to the way the plants project themselves. A very basic rule would be to divide those that like to bake, such as the *Iris germanica* and many of the tuberous rooted and bulbous types of the Middle East, and those from North America, Europe and Asia that prefer the ground deep and moisture-retentive. Of course, there are the rule-breakers, like our own *Iris foetidissima*, which has made its home in dry, calcareous woodland here in Britain, but the division is

PAGE 168
Iris fulva.

convenient. By and large, I have opted for the species that prefer our rich alluvial soil here in Peckham. I also grow the *Iris reticulata* in pots for bringing close to the house in late winter.

The hot spots here are few and carefully guarded and, with so much growth appearing later in the summer, even the hottest spaces become cool at ground level. Where the sun falls reliably to the ground along the path, the baking places are reserved for *Nerine bowdenii*, *Dierama* and *Amaryllis belladonna*, but I would not want to garden here without the winter illumination of the Algerian iris.

In the wild, *Iris unguicularis* grows in open, boulder-strewn landscapes where the ground is free-draining and conditions are tough. Cold is not so much the issue with cultivating them successfully, but free drainage and light are imperative. The poor ground that was previously depleted by the lime tree that I removed at the front of the house is the best I can do here to keep them happy. Old gardening books recommend growing them with brick rubble in the ground to emulate their origins, but they are happy as long as the ground drains freely and is low in nutrients. The evergreen foliage is kept in check in poor ground; in better conditions, it would become flabby, which would be at the expense of flowers. There is also enough light by the path for the knot of rhizomes to ripen over the summer. Ripening is what they need to produce their succession of winter flowers.

I am getting to know the dark-flowered 'Mary Barnard' here, though I have always grown the silvery blue 'Walter Butt' in the past. The latter has a little more to offer in terms of its delicate perfume, but I love them equally. 'Mary Barnard' has finer foliage, which is less prone to looking scruffy in the winter. The first flowers emerge as early as the winter solstice and often continue until March between the very coldest spells. They spear the strap-shaped leaves as buds no more than pencil thickness. If you pull them at this point and bring them inside, they unravel like a scroll in front of your eyes. This is also the best way to check their perfume, as January days are less than conducive to getting down on your hands and knees to bury your nose in a flower. Closely related, though happy in dappled shade and damper conditions, is *Iris lazica*. I do not know this plant well yet, having been introduced to it only recently by Peter Chappell of Spinners Nursery in Hampshire, but I intend to because winter iris are key in keeping the spirits up.

As the soil here tends to be damp in the winter, I have had most success with the perennial iris that like these conditions. *Iris* × *robusta* is a cross between the North American natives *I. virginica* and *I. versicolor*. 'Gerald Darby' is the selection I grow here, and the foliage

Iris japonica 'Ledger'.

Iris × *robusta* 'Gerald Darby'.

is easily as good as the flower. Iris foliage in spring is vivid, catching low light in the blades and rising vertically as a symbol of new life breaking ground. 'Gerald Darby' has the added benefit of foliage that is infused with an inky stain, the same colour as blue-black ink. The colouring stays in the young foliage until it is at least knee height, dissipating as the leaf expands and begins to arch over. It is retained in the flowering stems and travels up onto the base of the sky-blue flowers. The character of the plant is almost identical to our native yellow flag and, given a wet position or even submerged in water, it easily increases to a clump a metre across.

I grow *Iris chrysographes* 'Black Form' in a position previously occupied by an unnamed royal purple *Iris sibirica*, and I prefer their scale here, now that the garden is filling out. The two are similar in character, preferring the same cool ground, but *Iris chrysographes* is diminutive, with grass-like foliage that can easily be overwhelmed. It is important that this doesn't happen because they hate competition and will rapidly dwindle to nothing. That aside, the architecture of the leaf is something to be celebrated and it never looks better than when rising above its neighbours. I grow it with the delicate *Gillenia trifoliata*, and the pale lacy flowers are what the iris needs not to be lost in the shadows. The iris is tall and unbelievably elegant and, though the flowers last only a few days, I never begrudge them their brevity.

I saw the copper iris, *Iris fulva*, in Piet Oudolf's garden in Holland shortly after he replanted it. With typical generosity, he dug a piece up and gave it to me there and then. It has done well for me here, liking the cool ground between the *Hemerocallis*, and it is one of my all-time favourite plants for the couple of weeks that lead up to the longest day of the year. A plant of swamps and wet meadows in the US, it is adaptable, and the light shade it gets here makes up for the fact that it can get dry later in the summer. The leaves rise from an informal crown of rapidly colonizing rhizomes, and the flowers are held above the foliage at about knee height. I have interplanted them with *Baptisia australis*, which flowers at the same time, and the blue lupin flowers heighten the copper-brown of the iris flowers. In bud, they are the colour of ripening tomatoes, and a number of buds open in succession to keep you in flower for the best part of three weeks. Those that set seed make huge seed pods that are so heavy by autumn that they weigh the stem to the ground to be lost among foliage. When ripe, they rupture to reveal angular and strangely pulpy seed. I have not had success in germinating this yet, but I fully intend to, as the copper iris is a plant that I know I will want to grow forever.

Iris chrysographes 'Black Form'.

Gillenia trifoliata.

Summer

Combinations

My old friend Geraldine was one of the people responsible for fuelling my early enthusiasm in the garden. She lived along the lane and, from the age of five, I was a regular and frequent visitor. She was a naturalist at heart, and her garden was unkempt and idiosyncratic. The weeds were as much at home there as her considerable treasure-trove of plants, and everything had a history or an anecdote to bring it to life. It was a free and uninhibited garden that thrived because she knew how to place a plant where it would thrive.

On every day of the year, there would be a posy in a jam-jar on the kitchen table, in which the whole garden was distilled. Geraldine would pick the buds of *Iris unguicularis* on the shortest day of the year, to watch them open in the warmth. They would be joined by the last of the rosehips in December, and snowdrops, wintersweet and witch hazel as the winter deepened. In August, you might witness the transformation of a *Magnolia grandiflora*, from soapy bud to full-blown perfumed opulence, but you were just as likely to find it in its death throes – up close, each and every stage was fascinating. The posies were also gathered from walks and other people's gardens, and in them there must have been the germ of many an idea. Observing the plants at close quarters and out of context allowed her to look with a fresh eye and an open mind.

The construction of the posy is not something you should think about too much, for it is more the act of pulling things together for closer observation that is the objective. I have kept this tradition going and, now that the garden is over a decade old, I, too, am able to have a

PAGE 176
A posy of *Meconopsis cambrica*, *Geranium* 'Patricia', *Astrantia* 'Hadspen Blood', *Tulipa sylvestris*, *Papaver rupifragum* and *Bidens ferulifolia*.

jar of something on the windowsill every day of the year. I do it for several reasons, to be able to observe a plant up close and to appreciate its perfume or the way a flower changes as it goes through its life cycle. The posy enables you to keep an open mind and to take another look at combining colour, form or texture without having to worry about the practicalities. The posy is also a means of throwing together combinations of plants that are separated for some reason or other in the garden but which can be brought together in the pot.

Although I have moved many plants around the garden through discoveries coming together on the kitchen table, compatibility in the ground is essential if the aesthetic freedom of the posy is going to translate. I have already written about the importance of the right plant in the right place, but getting the most out of my space demands initiative and a constant curiostity.

Ipomoea purpurea 'Grandpa Otts'.

I garden intensively within the boundaries of my fences, so every square inch of soil is valuable. Layering the garden is key to being able to grow such a variety and wealth of plants. It also enables me to provide height and shade and a succession of interest so that each week of the year is catered for. Within each bed, there is a hierarchy of plant material that starts with the trees, shrubs or climbers. These provide year-round volume and, over time, they also contribute to the microclimate.

To give an example, the coyote willows grew fast in the early years of the garden, to provide a silvery backdrop. They covered for the slower-growing myrtle and *Rosa* x *odorata* 'Mutabilis' around them, and their lightness of foot also meant that I could grow things happily in their shade. They provided support for the self-sown morning glories, and the *Anemanthele lessoniana* (*Stipa arundinacea*) added evergreen foliage at their feet in the winter. In turn, and between the *Stipa*, the gaps are taken with a layering of seasonal interest. First to come are the *Paeonia mlokosewitschii* and the scarlet *Tulipa sprengeri*, which are happy to drop back into the shade of their companions later on, as they have been up early replenishing their storage organs. Next is a blaze of colour in the *Hemerocallis* 'Stafford' and *Crocosmia* 'Lucifer'. The bulbous *Lilium henryi* emerge among them and push clear of the perennials. I leave the occasional evening primrose to seed about, as there is usually a window opened up somewhere for an opportunistic biennial, and rely upon late-flowering *Salvia* and *Canna* x *ehemanii* to take me through to autumn. The fence here is covered with *Clematis* x *triternata* 'Rubromarginata'.

Canna x *ehemanii*.

This section of the garden offers colour, scent and textural contrast, as well as playing host to a wealth of insects and birds. It is also a part of the garden that has seen considerable change, with *Sambucus* 'Black Lace' replacing the coyote willows and altering the palette and conditions in the process. The posy helps in the process of adjusting to the change by keeping your mind open to the possibilities and the potential of what is possible. It is a microcosm in a jar, like a scrapbook of ideas that can be lived out in the ground.

Solstice

On the longest day, we make a point of sitting out under the hornbeam to witness the last of the light as the sky grows silvery. On a still evening, the swifts career through the leafy stretch of gardens that runs the length of the two streets that enclose them, screaming as they score the sky. Sometimes, and depending on the number of bugs that fill the air, there is a crossover with the bats, which flit low and silent through the hollows created by the vegetation. As the light drains to the west, the first buds of the evening primrose spring loose to mark the tilt into the second half of the year.

Oenothera biennis and *Salvia guaranitica* 'Blue Enigma' in the background.

You can feel the energy shifting towards the summer solstice, as all growth in the garden has been leading to this point, with foliage gathering in strength and volume to support the main flush of summer colour. This is yet to come, but the plants are vibrant and more verdant than they will be on the other side of the equinox, when the garden visibly shifts into another mode.

The *Crocosmia* 'Lucifer' exemplify what is happening, for they have been spearing skyward until now. The verticals of their pleated foliage is much of the reason that I grow them. Puncturing bare ground early in March, it is needle-thin, but it is not long before the sheaths expand and rise above their neighbours. Back-lit, for this is important if you are to make the most of them, they score a strong upright, which feels like it has been pulled skyward as much as it has been pushed from earth. In the week before the longest day, you notice that they have reached their summit and that the first flower buds are pushing the envelope of foliage apart. As they do, the plant begins to lean, in preparation to flower. It is important to have put the supporting metal hoops in place earlier if the clump is not to splay. In no time, and joined by a host of neighbours that are also readying, 'Lucifer' tilts its jagged flowers outward, buds popping flaming vermilion as high summer breaks.

Crocosmia 'Lucifer'.

The expectation of what is to come is always the most exciting aspect of this time of year. The *Eryngium agavifolium* crane up and away from the ground and are dramatic framed against the last of the light. The thimbles are visible, but yet to develop in fullness, and the stems are wand-like and shift in formation if there is a breeze. The hollyhocks have yet to tilt away from the horizontal, the buds lining the stems in readiness for action, and the *Hydrangea aspera* clutches its already formed flower buds like tightly clenched fists. They mark a later chapter in summer and weigh down the branches as they swell. This large-leaved hydrangea is one of my favourite late summer shrubs and, as it readies itself for later, it changes shape, lolling and leafy in the shade of the hornbeam.

In the week after the longest day, the neighbours' buddleia shows its first flowers. The balance tipped, the relationship between night and day initiates the later-blooming plants. The *Salvia guaranitica* 'Blue Enigma' and the pineapple sage are suddenly putting their energy not into leaf but into bud, and the *Tagetes* 'Cinnabar' are branching vigorously in readiness for high summer. As the volume builds, you hope that the balance you have struck this year will be one that hits all the notes you had in mind when the garden was down around your ankles in March.

Lilies

When I started gardening in the early Seventies, I remembered quite distinctly the lilies that my father grew in our back yard. To a beginner's eye, they claimed the position as the most exotic plants in the garden and, even then, I knew that they were otherworldly, with a sophistication that the dahlias in the vegetable patch fell short of.

First to flower at the tale end of June were the *Lilium regale*. I would later read E.H. Wilson's accounts of discovering them in a gorge in China, where they arched from the rocky hillsides in their hundreds, but Dad's were just as captivating in the oak tubs in the yard. I would eye the leaf mould in the spring for signs of growth and be gripped from the point at which the mahogany-red shoots emerged. They would rise up in just a matter of weeks, their fine whorl of foliage encasing an ascending stem, which slowed at about one to two metres. This was the point at which the embryonic buds would be visible in the tight ruff of foliage at the top. They emerged in a counter movement to the stem, separating, then moving out and then down as they gathered weight and volume. The deep red exterior would darken from green as the buds swelled. The buds broke one at a time to reveal the gentle sweep of the pure white interior, which led to a throat

Lilium regale.

splashed with gold. The stamens were dusted with saffron-coloured pollen, which stained your clothes and fingers. In a good year, there might be as many as twenty flowers to a stem, and their heady perfume would finger its way around the house and in through any open doors or windows.

These first encounters led to a small obsession in my teens, which today I have had to limit with the arrival of the dreaded lily beetle. Back then, it was confined to a small area of Surrey, but today it has spread across most of the country, and you have to be vigilant to avoid calamity. The scarlet beetles overwinter in the ground, so they are up on the first warm days in the spring. They go for the *Fritillaria* first before moving on to the lilies as they emerge in March. It is the grubs, not the brightly coloured beetles, that do the damage, and they lurk on the undersides of the leaf, covered in their own excrement and feeding as they go. You can spray your lilies with a systemic insecticide and overcome the problem, but I prefer the organic route and save the beneficial insects that would also succumb to chemical treatment by picking them off by hand.

Monitoring their attack is a time-consuming and daily exercise, but you soon get to know the habits of the beetles. They only come out in sunshine, seeming to rise at around 10 o'clock in the morning here, and are highly visible among the contrast of greenery. Any disturbance prompts them to jump, from the leaf and lie on their backs on the ground, perfectly camouflaged by their black undersides. This renders them invisible, so I have learned to cup my hand under the leaf to catch them as they jump and dispose of them swiftly beneath my heel. If they get to lay eggs, and they usually do, it is a messy exercise removing the grubs, but they will strip the foliage in a week if their numbers are sufficient and they are left unchecked. This weakens plants because they need their foliage to feed the bulb for next year.

Only a few lilies are truly perennial in the ground and sturdy enough to fend off ground slugs in winter, but it is the need to gain access to the lily beetle that now means I have most of mine in pots. They are grown in compost that I make up from the garden soil, with about a fifth of leaf mould worked into the mix. This keeps it free-draining and, when the bulbs are planted or divided in late winter, I set the bulbs in a layer of sharp grit to help the drainage and keep the ground slugs at bay.

The pots are moved around the garden according to the season. The first part of the summer sees them clustered in a group at the sunny end. I can monitor them easily here, and the early sunshine is good for replenishing the bulbs. As they come to bud, I move them to

Lilium speciosum var. *album*.

Lilium regale 'African Queen'.

the terraces so we can enjoy the transformation from bud to flower at closer quarters. After they are over, the pots are moved into the resting corner by the compost bins at the end of the garden. I give them a fortnightly seaweed feed to nurture next year's display, but the lily beetle will continue to prey upon them until the end of the summer, so I never forget to visit them, even when they are out of the way.

Lilium regale is the first to flower around the third week of June, and 'African Queen', a soft orange form with rust-coloured anthers, picks up shortly afterwards to keep the terraces perfumed until the end of July. The perfume is extraordinary, and it is hard to imagine high summer without it. Though *Lilium speciosum* is not scented, it is the last of the lilies to flower here during August and this extends the lily season into a month that can often feel as if it is hanging between summer and autumn.

Lilium speciosum 'Uchida'.

I grow two forms, both of which have pretty aching growth, widely spaced foliage, and flowers held apart from each other. *Lilium speciosum* var. *album*, the easiest to use of the two, is a clear, pure white. It has puckering marks where the spots are found in the non-albino form. I partner them with the moth-like *Nicotiana suaveolens*. 'Uchida' is a sugary pink selection, which is almost identical to var. *rubrum*. It has a cherry-pink ray along the centre of each of the reflexed petals, the spotting at the throat is dark pink and the anthers a rusty orange. On close observation, this makes an unlikely but appealing combination. 'Uchida' is infinitely nicer than 'Black Beauty', which has an enticing name that it doesn't live up to. The petals have something of the texture and colour of raw meat, and the plant has somehow lost the elegance of its parent.

Of those that I grow in the ground, close enough to the path to be easily tended, *Lilium pardalinum* var. *giganteum* is the first to flower at the beginning of July. In the wild in North America, the leopard lily is found in swampy areas, and I have seen it two metres or more in height where there is moisture. Although lilies like moisture, they need it to be moving through the ground and not sitting around, and this is why leaf mould is the perfect addition. Leaf mould keeps soil open while retaining the moisture. That said, *Lilium pardalinum* will tolerate heavier ground than many lilies, and I have it planted in the dampest part of the garden here. Though slow to establish, its curious, stoloniferous bulbs are now bulking up well and have formed quite a clump just below the surface. The growth is spectacular and fast in early summer, rising up, one whorl of foliage at a time, to the height of the *Euphorbia mellifera*. The acid green foliage of the euphorbia has given way to rust-orange flower heads by the time the lily's turk's-cap flowers reflex. They are dark orange-red with a yolk-yellow throat

Lilium pardalinum var. *giganteum*.

spotted with brown, and the anthers are held elegantly away from the body of the flower by curving pale green filaments.

The *Lilium henryi* are at their height of flower in mid-July. They have been completely reliable in the ground here, and in good years have as many as thirty flowers to a stem. The colour is a soft, pure orange, with subtle, puckered maroon markings. The anthers are also orange and dangle on the ends of pale green filaments. The growth is arching, and plants need gentle staking from early in the season. With the exception of the chrome-yellow 'Citronella', all the lilies need staking if they are not to succumb to wind and rain when they are heavy with flower. This is an easy exercise with the metal hoops, which still allow them their grace. I leave all but the *Lilium regale* to go to seed because I like the seed heads, but I wonder if removing them really makes the difference it is supposed to. I can see the energy they put into the seed is considerable, but the seed heads are better to look at in the autumn than a naturally elegant plant beheaded.

Lilium henryi.

Zenith

In the last week of June and the first of July, the garden looks its best, and if there is a moment of perfection, this is probably it. A friend who was staying over this period asked if it had been planned to happen like this. She likened it to a firework display where the raw materials for the display had been laid out in the knowledge of how they would come together once the touch paper was ignited. I took the compliment. You never look at your own garden in such an unjudgmental manner, knowing all of the imperfections that got the garden to this point and the flaws that were yet to come. Of course, every year is different, but this particular climax, the first push of summer colour, is one that shifts the garden onto a different level.

The underpinning of green gives way to a wave of free, uninhibited colour and, in the spirit of experimentation, I wouldn't have it any other way. It increases daily as the main flush of summer perennials comes together and one combination builds upon another. Some of these are old combinations and personal favourites that I want to live with in my own garden. It is important to witness a combination from beginning to end and to know how it will evolve over time. The majority, though, are new or chance happenings, where things come together unexpectedly.

Although there is a freedom in the use of colour here, the principle tends to be that the softer colours – the mauves, blues, whites and pale yellows – are found in the shade or within leafiness. You only have to think of a bluebell wood in dappled light to understand that mauve, blue and blue-purple hover or glow in shade, while they are lost or bleached out in the sun. White and yellow bring a sparkle to the shadows and illuminate places that could all too easily be sombre, but the brilliant white of *Zantedeschia aethiopica* reflects too much light out in the sun. I prefer their cool elegance here among the *Molinia* in the shade of the bamboo. Yellow can also flare if placed in the full glare of sunshine, acting as a distraction rather than a highlight. This can work to advantage but, as a rule, I use the softer yellows like the *Thalictrum flavum* and evening primrose in the sun. The water lilies that rise to the surface in the copper are a good use of yellow and they flower less freely in the dappled shade of the hornbeam. Each flower becomes a treasure and lights up the deck, even when the sun is behind the clouds.

Hotter colours with a deeper vibrancy and punch are usually placed in the lightest, brightest areas, where the light only magnifies their effect, but I break all of these rules repeatedly. I feel that I am able to do this because the greater majority of plants in the garden are fairly close to the species, so the colour is pure and unadulterated by breeding. You never see clashing colour in a meadow because the colour is pure and the flowers small. The garden here works on the same principle, placing the colour where it works to best advantage and using it like paint, where a contrast or complement is needed.

Although the colour in the garden has to read as a cohesive composition (so that you can take in the wider picture and not be pulled in all directions on first impression), it is important that you also come upon the unexpected. The plants that are used en masse set the tone, but the incidentals, such as the self-seeding evening primrose, turn up the volume and inject friction and spontaneity. *Oenothera biennis* is a plant of wastelands and you have to be careful not to let it dominate, as it is prolific. The clear, pure yellow is also surprisingly powerful and it can easily overwhelm the soft, primrose-yellow of *Alcea rugosa*. I keep them apart now that I have learned that lesson, but I love the clarity of yellow and I use it to draw the eye down the length of the garden. Even though the yellow flowers are often soft, small or sparse, a smattering of *Bidens ferulifolia* is like buttercups in the sunshine and will inject a particular energy where it is needed.

Hemerocallis 'Stafford' with *Crocosmia* 'Lucifer' is a coupling that I grow for sentimental reasons, and both plants came from the Barn Garden at Home Farm. They provide the dominant colour at the beginning of the flowering wave, and the red is powerful where they

Thalictrum lucidum.

Alcea rugosa.

PAGE 185
Zantedeschia aethiopica and
Molinia caerulea subsp. *arundinacea*
'Transparent'.

PAGES 186–7
Midsummer, with *Lilium pardalinum*
var. *giganteum* to the left and *Geranium*
'Patricia' spilling over the path.

PAGES 188–9
Lilium 'Citronella' with *Geranium*
'Ann Folkard'.

cluster together. I let this happen close to the deck, but it is important that this weight of red breaks away into the surrounding planting through the dots of *Potentilla* 'Gibson's Scarlet'. This appears on both sides of the path, and the red is pure zinging scarlet, with the flowers small enough to act like drops of blood. Being small, they enliven the dull maroon haze of the *Sanguisorba* 'Tanna', and the darker, duller red allows me to then inject the pinks.

The silvery pink *Dierama pulcherrimum* arch over the path from both sides in the first half of July and, though they are sometimes bothersome when in full flower, I like them suspended in the space of the path. They hate competition and rapidly weaken in a competitive situation because they like the air and the light to be able to reach the basal clump of foliage. They also hate to be moved, and the best plants here are the self-sown seedlings. The angel's fishing rods are part of a rosy cluster here with magenta *Lychnis coronaria* and carmine *Dianthus carthusianorum*.

Taking a facet of colour from one plant and using it as a lead for a companion can be a good rule of thumb. The silvery casings of the *Dierama* work well with the reflective *Eryngium giganteum* around them and the mauve in the *Verbena bonariensis* chimes well with the darker *Cleome hassleriana* (syn. *spinosa*) 'Violet Queen'. The browns and rust of the *Bupleurum longifolium* take your eye through from the marbling of the *Podophyllum*, but these colours are just as interesting in contrast. I like to play with opposites so that there is tension. I also have chrome-yellow *Centaurea macrocephala* alongside the *Lychnis*, primrose-yellow *Alcea rugosa* with the *Cleome*, and *Lilium* 'Citronella' with the dark-eyed *Geranium* 'Ann Folkard'. Certain plants play hard in the mix, and the acidic green of the *Euphorbia cornigera* is important for its duration. It is only just coming into flower when the scarlet *Tulipa sprengeri* are out, but is a metre high and making the vermilion of the *Crocosmia* vibrate by this time of the year. Later in the season, as things get looser, it will still be there to deepen the blue of the *Salvia gauranitica*, which without its unexpected partner is half as blue and half as appealing.

Potentilla 'Gibson's Scarlet'.

Lychnis coronaria and
Dianthus carthusianorum.

Hemerocallis

The *Hemerocallis* (day lilies) are known as 'doers', being deer-proof, rabbit-tolerant and as happy out in the sun as they are in the shade. Consequently, they have been seized upon by nurserymen (American, mostly), who have developed an overwhelming range of several

PAGES 190–1
High summer, with *Hemerocallis* 'Stafford', *Oenoethera biennis*, *Crocosmia* 'Lucifer', *Thalictrum lucidum*, *Salvia guaranitica* 'Blue Enigma', *Lilium henryi* and *Alcea rugosa* in the distance.

PAGE 192
Hemerocallis 'Stafford'.

hundred varieties. In my opinion, the greater majority are, unfortunately, not worth bothering with, as they have lost their grace through being dwarf or double, or from having their colour combinations meddled with unnecessarily to suit fashion. If you have been lucky enough to see the wild day lily in its natural habitat, as I have in Japan, you will understand why I feel so strongly that simple is best. *Hemerocallis dumortieri* is a pure, unadulterated gold, and the flowers hover, never too many at a time, on wire-thin stems. In Japan, they grow in light woodland or on the fringes of it, and their strappy foliage is lost among the meadow grasses, which hide them until they flower. Put your nose to the flower and they yield a sweet perfume.

Hemerocallis lilioasphodelus.

Hemerocallis lilioasphodelus, which is similar to *H. dumortieri* but a softer shade of yellow, was one of the first species from which the breeding took place, but today many of the cultivars have lost their scent. This species is the first to show in the garden here and they make their way skyward together with the white *Allium*, which flower in tandem from the middle of May. My plants are orphans from a Chelsea Flower Show garden, where I included them in homage to those that I had seen on the edge of woodland in Hokkaido. They made their way to Peckham in the back of the car, bedraggled after the show garden was pulled apart but still with enough bud to see out the end of the month.

Whereas the majority of the garden cultivars are completely reliable in their clump-forming nature and stay put in one spot for decades without division, this delicate day lily creeps gently by sending out underground stolons, moving unobtrusively through its neighbours. I doubt that this behaviour would ever be a problem because the nature of the plant is to accommodate itself in company. Though it will not mind a little shade, the key to combining it successfully is to associate it with plants that will never completely overwhelm the basal foliage. I have planted mine towards the front of the bed with *Aquilegia* 'Yellow Star' and *Bupleurum longifolium*. The flowers rise up to waist height and, although each lasts only a day, they are present for the best part of three weeks, with a smattering of gold and a delicious scent.

Aquilegia 'Yellow Star' and *Bupleurum longifolium*.

There are two groups of *Hemerocallis* 'Stafford' that come a whole month later, the first flowers opening around the longest day of the year, the last withering at the end of July. They were lifted from the Barn Garden at Home Farm and are one of the plants that I would take with me should I leave this garden. Though they are without scent, they bring with them an entirely different mood, which pumps up the colour in July. The display begins slowly but, within a week of starting, there are so many flowers out at any one time that it is impossible to count them. 'Stafford' is the best of the reds in my book, and saved from being too intense because the petals are finer than many of the cultivars and reflex to throw open their vivid gold interior. The stems are long and graceful, and a small group of three to five plants, closely spaced thirty centimetres apart, can easily fill the span of your outstretched arms. The exterior of the buds is a rich greeny-yellow, which fades to a deep rust-red, the predominating colour of the exterior. There are six petals, the three widest often streaked with a slash of the same yellow that burns in the throat. The anthers are dusted with gold.

Hemerocallis citrina x *ochroleuca.*

The petals are rather fleshy and can look unsightly if left after their day of glory so, to keep them looking smart for the duration of the flowering period, I deadhead them every third morning or so, staining my hands a bloody red in the process. This is deeply satisfying, with yesterday's flowers coming away with a clean snap at the base of the seed pod. Towards the end of the flowering, I leave those that have been pollinated to produce seed heads because they make interesting winter skeletons.

I first came across *Hemerocallis altissima* one August at Great Dixter, where they were proving themselves by flowering late. The small, pale lemon flowers stood on stems that were easily as tall as me and, being night-flowering and scented, I imagined them among the evening primroses. I have failed to get them to flower here, despite moving them around the garden, because they dislike growth around the basal clump. It is a pity and I have not given up, but I have a smaller, yellow-flowering form called *H. citrina* x *ochroleuca* that flowers earlier in July. It is similar to another favourite, *H.* 'Hyperion' (which I would grow if I had the room), in that the petals are finely rayed like a line drawing. The linearity of the flower means that deadheading can be sidestepped because the withering is almost as interesting as the buds that are yet to come. Again, there is scent if you bring them to your nose.

Despite my failure to get *H. altissima* to flower, the day lilies are an incredibly easy group of plants. They are pest-free, except for the odd slug attack in their youth, but they are prone to *Hemerocallis* gall midge, which, if you have it in your area, will lay its eggs in the buds where the larvae feed. The buds swell and distort as the grubs develop, causing what an American friend refers to as 'fat bud'. The best method of control is to pick off the affected buds and destroy them to prevent the grubs developing.

Ecosystem

The open space between the houses on our street and those behind us continues regardless of the boundaries that frame our city lives. Sandwiched between the two terraces running up and down the hill to either side, the gardens form a corridor that is only separated from the park at the top by a crossroad. The trees that line the road touch in the middle, and the park is bordered by the railway line, with its frayed embankments covered in buddleia and willowherb. The tracks connect a ribbon of scrub that leads into town and on to the river at London Bridge, but in the other direction they run into an ever-expanding weight of suburban greenery, and the countryside is not far beyond.

A bee on *Salvia guaranitica* 'Black and Blue'.

In the greater scheme of things, our self-imposed boundaries are merely cosmetic, and we are often amazed by the wildlife that arrives in the garden. I sleep in the back room at the top of the house and regularly lean out of the window to ponder the green acreage of which we are a part. There is an airy view of St Giles's church steeple in Camberwell, with trees peeking above the houses, which soften and blur the hard edges. The gardens sprawl into each other with shrubs that do not know the limit of walls and fences and lolloping hedges, connecting and interconnecting the spaces like loose handwriting. And above all of this is the network of trees – sycamore, ash, cherry, oak and holly, as well as the ornamentals – which provide a habitat and lifeline for the birds. The hairline fracture of fences and the relatively modest weave of roads that run through and underneath this weight of vegetation are of little consequence to them, the bees or, for that matter, the lily beetles.

The gardens to either side of us go in and out of use according to who is living there. At the moment, the creeping thistle and *Allium triquetrum* are running under the fence from the south side, where the garden has been left untouched by the tenants. To the other side, the buddleia, bindweed and brambles mark a garden that has been disregarded by the intermittent tenants. Further up, there is a sycamore grove and a longer tenancy of neglect. In many ways, this is not so dissimilar to a coppice system in the countryside, with the vegetation opening up and closing as it is cleared and allowed to regrow in rotation. These habitats are some of the richest areas for wildlife because they are always in flux, and the status quo is never overwhelmed by any one species. And so it is with our gardens in the city. Each environment contributes to the next, whether the garden is neglected or tended.

Though you might think that gardens gone native is the reason that the wildlife is as rich as it is in the city, it is actually the diversity of plants and habitats that gives it such potential. Whereas a native hedgerow or verge has a limited flowering season in the countryside, the range of plants that are grown in domestic gardens is far wider, giving a better measured and longer flowering season. *Viburnum*, hellebores and *Pulmonaria* provide nectar for the early bumblebees, and late-blooming asters flower well after our native plants have gone to seed. Although 'low-maintenance' gardens may not seem to offer up much in the way of diversity, compare them to the monocrop farming methods of the countryside, where hedges have been removed and chemicals applied to keep the weeds and the bugs at bay, for mile after square mile. From my top windows, it looks like the city has plenty to offer.

Of course, there are the unwanted guests: the vine weevils, which deposit their silent, deathly grubs in the pots, the scarlet lily beetle and the solomon's seal sawfly, to name just three. Every few years, something new arrives as an 'exotic' introduction from mainland Europe. Rosemary beetle appeared here three years ago, and in five years the harlequin ladybird has all but erased our native two-spot beetle by cleaning up its larvae and the supply of aphids. A monstrous scale insect, the size of a thumbnail, has also arrived on the wisteria. I have meticulously painted each and every leaf with methylated spirits and, so far, kept it at bay. I can keep on top of most things in a garden this size without having to resort to spraying. The lily beetle is disposed of daily before they lay their eggs, and I apply nematodes to control the grubs of the vine weevils. I have to put up with the red spider mite if it hits the *Brugmansia* and the *Euphorbia* in a dry summer. Daily spraying with water helps, as they hate the wet. So far, I do not have the bamboo mite that the RHS is threatening, but I guess it won't be long because, with international plant exports and climate change, things are set to change.

As gardeners we just have to adapt. Eventually, I will have to get rid of my beloved *Impatiens tinctoria* – year after year, the capsid bugs have attacked the buds as they are developing. A late summer-flowerer in any case, the second crop of flowers that develops after the grubs have departed always gets caught by the frost and it makes me question whether it is worth the effort to keep it. In another garden, the problems will be different, and I have grown this *Impatiens* elsewhere without any trouble.

The local foxes have a den under a huge Victorian conifer several doors up, and it is impossible to keep them out of the garden. I see

A hoverfly on *Veronicastrum virginicum* 'Album'.

them sauntering across the neighbouring garage roof in broad daylight and have watched them scale a three-metre fence and even nimbly squeeze through trellis without seeming to touch the sides. They are wily and show it by defecating in the centre of the path or the middle of a step, on the handle of my lance or in a pot, and I think they know exactly what they are doing. The dirty nappies and fast-food cartons I find at the back of the borders are the least of the problem if they decide they are going to romp in the planting – I have come out some mornings to see the day lilies flattened just as they are forming their buds. This is heartbreaking but you have to hold your breath and count to ten when it happens. Placing obstacles on their route as soon as it becomes apparent seems to be the best method of discouragement. I prevent bad habits developing by plugging holes as soon as they appear under the plants and make their sunbathing spots out of bounds with bamboo cloches.

I deliberately encourage the garden to have frayed edges, and the blackbirds nest safe from the cats in the tangle of ivy and *Rosa* 'Cooperi' at the end. Before they died, the coyote willows provided another favourite wildlife moment, as they were a favourite feeding ground of the long-tailed tits, which would dart, chattering, from branch to branch, hidden by the shimmering leaves. Hiding places are important, so that the birds can easily be out of cats' reach. The cats are the reason that I feed the birds only in the coldest weather, taking the risk that they are canny enough to use the water vessels only when the cats are lazing around inside. This is another reason that I leave winter skeletons standing, so that the hungry birds have somewhere to hide, while also providing hibernacula for insects.

The swifts, which careen screeching through the clearings, and then the bats, which overlap in the gloaming hour, come to feed on the wealth of bugs in the air. The midges and the flies are the result of the growth in the gardens. After clearing the undergrowth in the first year here and reducing it back to the bare bones of the fences, it was no surprise that, for the first couple of years, I was plagued by aphids. The ecology and the airspace above me were barren and the roses furred along their stems with greenfly. Now that the ecology is better balanced, I hold out if there is an attack, as it is usually cleared by the tits, the lacewings, the ladybirds and the hoverfly larvae. The organic principles do work, and in all but the mildest winters, when the aphids emerge before the hoverflies, I rarely resort to preventative soap washes.

I plant a wealth of nectar-rich plants to attract insects. Flat umbellifers such as fennel are perfect as landing pads for hoverflies,

A moth caterpillar on *Valeriana officinalis*.

and the *Eryngium* attract four or five different types of bee alone, as well as pollen beetles. On a hot summer day, their domes are alive with buzzing. The wealth of growth has also introduced a stillness here, and there are now butterflies frequenting the garden that were never here in the years immediately after it was cleared. We are now visited regularly by speckled woods, holly blues, painted ladies, commas, small tortoiseshells and peacocks, as well as the zebra-striped wood tiger moth and, more rarely, the hummingbird hawk moth, both of which fly by day.

Stag beetles are regulars in June, hatching from the woodpiles I have left behind the bamboo at the end. Appearing, almost without fail, on the hottest day of the month, they look so ancient and foreign, rustling through the leaf litter before launching themselves on their unsteady, meandering flight. And there are dragonflies and damselflies, which, I guess, lay their eggs in someone else's pond, or perhaps have travelled this far from nearby Burgess Park. I have never found their grubs when clearing the water lilies in the copper, but wouldn't be surprised to find that they were there. Each discovery makes me only more committed to keeping the balance tilted in their direction and more willing to take the rough with the smooth.

Butterfly eggs on *Pelargonium* 'Stadt Bern'.

Transparency

Aspiring to a garden that looks harmonious and in balance is a fine goal to have, but the process of getting there is the greater part of the pleasure. The garden here is dense with plants, and I am the first to admit that there are way too many of them even for a space this large. As it's my own garden, I am allowed to break the rules, but it is a balancing act to make them sit well in each other's company. Colour is used to move your eye through the planting, while texture and scale of foliage allow it to alight on something calm and contrasting. Some plants, such as the evergreen myrtle, the box and the bamboo, add weight and neutrality. They are the full stop and prevent your eye from travelling further, but I rely heavily upon transparency, or a series of veils, as a lighter counterpoint.

Veils do several things but, most importantly, they conceal without completely hiding. They allow your mind to fill the gaps and to play with what lies beyond. I became interested in this as a concept while looking at meadows. From a distance (or if you look up and out when standing in one), a meadow reads as a single rolling mass that hugs the contours of the topography, but when you refocus your eye more closely, you are intensely aware that there are thousands of components making up the whole. Like the dots in a pointillist painting, up close the buttercups, orchids and knapweeds are as bright as any flower might be. However, set among the hazy gauze of grasses, their brightness never competes but floats in a sea of green.

Ornamental grasses are one way of working a veil into a planting because their stems are as thin as wire and barely visible at first glance. Their flowers are often tiny, held in sprays so fine they register as one. Look closely and it is hard to identify the colour of the flower, but en masse it resembles a wash, which sets a tone. However, I am using grasses less, or at least with more discretion, in ornamental plantings. Despite their ability to imbue a naturalistic mood, many have a strong character, which, like their giant cousin, the bamboo, dominates the mood. I have chosen the quieter grasses for the garden here and have stuck to my rule never to use more than three in any one place, to avoid confusion. A meadow will be made up of tens of grasses but, if you look at the whole, at first you will read only the differences between a few.

The *Miscanthus* have been and gone from this garden. They are a good example of a grass that demands your attention, which is one of the reasons I removed them. I favour grasses that make a lighter impression, such as the aforementioned *Milium effusum* 'Aureum'. I am still experimenting, though, and *Panicum* are the latest group on trial here. I like the silvery-toned *P. virgatum* 'Heavy Metal' very much, but suspect that the ground is too rich for these North American prairie grasses and that they would be best treated a little mean once established, to keep them stout.

I have a group of *Molinia caerulea* subsp. *arundinacea* 'Transparent' beyond the deck, to veil what lies beyond them in the furthest reaches of the garden. They start to make their presence felt from July. I first saw this magical grass in the gardens of the landscape architect Mien Ruys in Holland, where she grew them with space around them, so that you could see the movement in them when the breeze caught the inflorescence. Here, they eventually have a reach of at least two metres across, and we have to squeeze our way past them by the end of September. It is not an ideal situation, particularly after it has rained, but they offer far too much to cause you to worry about getting wet on the way to the compost. The movement in the flowers marks the stillness of the box beside them.

A veil can take many forms and, much earlier in the year when covered in flower and tiny leaves, the *Cercis canadensis* 'Forest Pansy' stops your eye from seeing the end of the garden from the basement.

PAGE 201
Cosmos astrosanguineus and *Pelargonium* 'Stadt Bern'.

PAGES 202–3
High summer border, with *Dierama pulcherrimum*, *Eryngium agavifolium* and *E. giganteum* and *Sanguisorba* 'Tanna'.

PAGES 204–5
Tetrapanax papyrifer 'Rex'.

PAGES 206–7
Hydrangea aspera Villosa Group, *Geranium* 'Patricia' and emerging *Persicaria amplexicaulis* 'Alba'.

PAGES 208–9
The pots at the end of the garden are planted with an annually changing selection of hot-coloured perennials and annuals.

PAGES 210–11
Datura inoxia and *Tagetes* 'Cinnabar'.

PAGES 212–13
Pruning the wisteria.

PAGES 214–15
Late summer with *Bidens ferulifolia*, *Eryngium agavifolium*, *Alcea rugosa* and *Verbena bonariensis*.

It creates a sense of mystery, which makes you want to know what is beyond. For several years, the coyote willow also provided one without cutting off the end of the garden. It worked because its foliage is tiny and held lightly in the air. Through growing it, I have set myself the task of finding more plants with a similar quality.

The *Verbena bonariensis* is an obvious contender and, though I love it, I rarely have more than a dozen plants in any one year. They move around by self-seeding, and the art is in leaving them where they can occupy space while seeming not to. In common with the grasses, they have wire-thin stems, which allow you to look through their delicate cage of growth, but let them seed too freely and their seemingly fragile nature can become too dominant. As a pioneer, they like open, disturbed soil and will take over given the chance. The vibrant lavender of the flowers is also quite sharp and demanding – another reason to use them sparingly.

Cephalaria dipsacoides has a similar quality to the verbena, with a fine basal clump of growth and delicate primrose-yellow flowers. But whereas the verbena is ramrod-straight and rigid in feel, the *Cephalaria* has a gangly quality, and the flowers dance in the wind on wiry stems. This plant seeds freely here, though it is light on its feet and half the weight of the earlier, once-flowering *Cephalaria gigantea*. The pale flowers, so similar to scabious at first sight, appear in high summer, but they are out for the whole of August and will often be there with the last of the spidery *Cleome*.

Although I have only one plant here on trial, I have had great success with the thimble-flowered *Eryngium ebracteatum* in gardens with an open, airy disposition. At first sight, you might think this thistle was a *Sanguisorba*, with its plum-coloured pinheads held on fine stems – one day, I plan to grow more of it as a base through which other plants can come and go. The thimble-flowered *Sanguisorba* 'Tanna' is very happy here and does much the same task of unifying the plants that travel through it up the length of the path. Each flower head is tiny but en masse they throw a wash of colour along the path and keep the planting feeling light on its feet and unified. The effect they provide is amplified by the *Dierama pulcherrimum* above them, which form a curtain that you must walk through to reach the deck.

The aptly named *Gaura lindheimeri* 'Whirling Butterflies' work in much the same way, injecting a complementary lightness to the surrounding planting. Their tiny white flowers are delicate and hard to pin down, and I let the plants arrive unannounced. They have colonized the hot, free-draining places in the path where they like to seed, and they help me blur the boundaries.

PAGE 216
Cleome hassleriana (syn. *spinosa*) 'Violet Queen'.

Pelargonium

It would be hard to imagine gardening without *Pelargonium*, and I have experimented over the years to find my favourites. The choice is bewildering, but I have quickly narrowed them down to the single-flowered varieties, as they are less prone to rotting than the doubles in our wet summers. Without too much imagination, you can also picture the singles in the wild and, as I am also a purist in terms of colour, I like the geranium-red to fulfil its role as an injection of energy. A pure, geranium-red, consisting of more orange than pink, is hard to beat, and I put them with an inferno of colour in the pots grouped at the end of the garden. The display changes every year, but there are stalwarts I am never without. The *Pelargonium* 'Stadt Bern' are usually joined by a vigorous *Tagetes* called 'Cinnabar', given to me by Fergus Garrett, Head Gardener at Great Dixter. The petals are a mahogany velvet above, with ochre undersides, and they make a good combination with *Ipomaea lobata*. The *Ipomaea* is grown up canes to lick and flame in the air.

Tagetes 'Cinnabar', with *Albizia julibrissin* 'Summer Chocolate' in the background.

The five pots of 'Stadt Bern' are plants I bought over a decade ago from New Covent Garden Flower Market, but there are various cuttings waiting in the wings should the originals fail. I take cuttings in high summer with semi-ripe cuttings of *Salvia discolor* and other plants that I want to increase or overwinter as backup. I remove the flowers to save energy for root production and make a clean cut under the leaf junction. The cuttings are dipped in hormone rooting powder and set several to a pot in a free-draining mix of fifty-fifty loam and sharp grit. They are kept in a cool corner of the frame until they are rooted, leaving a good two months to fill the pot before the onset of autumn. A well-established plant has the resistance to endure the winter in the comparatively lower light levels of the garage.

Pelargonium 'Mrs Pollock'.

The half-hardy cuttings will be overwintered on the dry side alongside their parents – they are kept dry to promote a state of half-dormancy. They will be 'started' again in March by increasing the watering so that they are leafed up and ready for summer. Without doubt, the red of 'Stadt Bern' is a colour of highest summer, and there is an awkward moment in late May when the first flowers are at odds with their softer surroundings. I keep them on the terrace up by the house until it feels like the summer is properly with us before allowing them centre stage further down the garden.

For several years in a row, I played with the craziness of *Pelargonium* 'Mrs Pollock'. The single tangerine-red flowers are almost an aside, for it is the madness of the zonal leaf markings that sets this plant apart. Yellow, lime, maroon and brown appear in the leaf and, for a while, I loved the touch of anarchy they provided. But, as with anything too demanding, their constant clamour became tiresome, so I left the plants out in the frost one November to wipe the slate clean for the next year. One day I will grow them again, but I have in mind a sunny corner tucked away, so that you can pass by, admire them for a moment and then continue on your way somewhere else.

The on-line Woottens of Wenhaston catalogue has made it easy to experiment, and I now have quite a collection of species and scented-leaved *Pelargonium*. In truth, there have been as many failures as there have been successes, which is not surprising because these plants could not be further from the arid lands of South Africa whence they hail. They demonstrate their distaste for our damp climate here by sulking. Tantalizingly, *P.* 'Ardens' flowered for me once, with dark, bloody specks held in space. The white-flowered *P. triste* did the same, its thrown-back flowers luminous and scented at night, but then they moped and there is not much room here for plants that are out of sorts. What they require is the shelter of a glasshouse or a fully lit sunny windowsill, where the atmosphere is dry. Not all the species are difficult and, if you have to grow them outside without protection in summer, it is simply a question of finding the plants that prefer our climate. Those that do well are grown in a loam-based compost with plenty of grit and a fairly low fertility, so that they don't go to leaf. I give them liquid seaweed feed as and when they show signs of needing it.

Pelargonium sidoides have proven to be completely reliable, and my plants now predate moving here. They have formed a tight network of short, woody stems, and the penny-sized, grey-green leaves are low down and barely scented. Though they have been fickle some years and waited until August to throw out the first flower, most years the blooms come with the first heat of the summer. Each is tiny and the darkest maroon-purple, which appears almost black in bright sunshine. I grow them on the hot slate bench in the brightest part of the garden, where they are joined by a rota of scented-leaved *Pelargonium*, clove-scented pinks and bright *Salvia greggii*. I use tiny pieces of the leaves of *P.* 'Attar of Roses' to perfume summer ice cream and, though I haven't yet worked out how to use it, the lemon-scented 'Mabel Grey' is mouthwatering. Even though the leaves are delicately netted, *P. denticulatum* 'Filicifolium' has a powerful aromatic perfume of oils and musk. *Pelargonium* 'Peppermint Lace' is grey-leaved and rangy, with a pure white flower and a scented leaf that is clean and refreshing.

Salvia greggii.

Pelargonium 'Peppermint Lace'.

Down in the shade of the house, I have chosen varieties that can take less sunshine. 'Purple Unique' would flower better with more light, but the cooler conditions are conducive to the production of foliage. An upright plant by nature, this has the most strongly perfumed leaf of all those that I grow. It can scent a considerable orbit with the muskiness of church incense on a damp, warm day. Brush past it and you will carry it with you on your clothes or fingers. The flowers are a powerful, vivid mauve with a dark eye.

Pelargonium 'Purple Unique'.

I group several aromatic *Pelargonium* together at the base of the wisteria because this is the first place you pass as you go into the garden. The large-leaved *P. papilionaceum* is happiest here, as it is found on the edge of woodland in the wild. It grows tall, with woody limbs bearing simple leaves as wide as an outstretched palm. If you have room to keep the plant through the winter without having to cut it back, it will bear sprays of violet-pink flowers in the spring, which are as delicate as butterflies – hence the specific name. *Pelargonium tomentosum* is also a woodlander, happy to sprawl and scramble if it is given the space. The peppermint-scented foliage is completely covered with a thick downy pile, which is as soft as velvet. The white flowers, which come in early summer, are tiny and inconsequential, but I overlook them in favour of the leaves. They invite you to reach out to stroke them as you pass and, in doing so, you perform a little ritual that engages you, marks you and allows you to enter the garden in a changed frame of mind.

Climbers

Climbers know no boundaries. Their modus operandi is to reach for the light, and most stop only when they have done so. Many are ruthless about how they go about it, to the point that they eventually overwhelm their host and bring it crashing down before setting off to conquer yet more territory. They go about this with various adaptations. Some have aerial roots, which in the case of the *Parthenocissus* have developed into curious-looking suckering pads; others twine their stems around their support, often choking it in the process. In the case of the clematis, the leaf stalks twist to get a purchase, while vines have adapted leaf petioles in their ambition to get above the rest.

Scandent climbers make their way to the top of the canopy by flinging out limbs over their host. These limbs are far too long and far-reaching to support themselves, but the system works as long as the host is slower off the mark than the interloper. In the case of the rambling roses, the rangy limbs are also equipped with thorns that are angled downward to gain and retain a purchase. If you have ever tried to pull a rose out of a tree from underneath, you will see how the thorns resist like a grapple, but climb into the tree and pull away from the centre of gravity and the limbs come away easily. There is no such thing as an easy rambling rose and you need to take precautions to ensure you escape unscathed.

Knowing the nature of your climbers and how they take advantage of their situation is key to their use. Nearly all climbers, however vigorous once they have a hold, need help in the early stages or they will flounder around on the ground. If they are not given extra help, it might take a whole growing season to reactivate their will to ascend, so putting in a support system when you plant is essential. Self-clinging climbers such as *Parthenocissus*, *Hedera* and *Schizophragma* need early support as much as the climbers that require a framework. Unless they are in contact with the surface on which they are to climb, they will fail to produce aerial roots.

As I do not have any trees that are large enough to send climbers into, the fences and the walls are wired to create a framework. The powerful growth hormones in their tips mean that most climbers want to ascend vertically, but training growth horizontally removes the ambition to ascend and promotes a reaction in the plant to produce flowering wood. In the case of wisteria, this is what you are after, and even roses will flower more freely on growth that is arched away from the vertical. Vine eyes, which keep wires away from the walls and fences, are run from knee height to the furthest I dare ascend on a ladder. The 'rungs' between the wires are no more than thirty centimetres apart so that it is easy to make connections from one to the next. I feed twiggy wood from the bamboos or the hornbeam behind the wires where climbers need help to jump from one to the next.

You would expect to know the extent and vigour of a tree before planting it, and the same can be said of your climbers. Their vigour should match their position and, unless you can afford the space to let a climber go, or have the trees in which to let them loose without fear of losing the tree, you are bound to an annual round of pruning. Pruning keeps the wisteria out of the gutters, the Virginia creeper from lifting the tiles, and neighbourly relations intact.

Neighbours and climbers also need careful matching, and I know from bitter experience that it is unwise to assume that everyone feels the same way about growth. The neighbours to one side remain inside

Vitis coignetiae, Parthenocissus henryana and *Hedera colchica.*

for all but one or two days a year, and the days they are out it is with a strimmer, to keep the weeds in check. Except for the creeping thistle that ventures under the fence, I am happy for this to be the case. The birds and the insects like the neighbouring tumble of growth while it is allowed its reign, but the strimmer is used with a zero-tolerance policy to vegetation and this is where I came a cropper last summer.

The high-pitched whir of the engine and the smell of freshly cut vegetation should have been the trigger to check the 'Mermaid' rose. I knew it was hanging over the other side of the fence, but I was lost in another world of writing. It wasn't until a couple of hours later that I noticed the *Vitis coignetiae* was wilting. It had formed an elbow that rested on the top of the fence before leaping on and up into the hornbeam but, when I went to investigate the cause, I saw that this main artery had been severed and was literally pumping sap. When I went around to speak to the neighbour, trying to hold back a storm, his garden was reduced to a dust bowl, and the 'Mermaid' had been sheared back in line. All I could do was ask that he give me warning next time and learn to avert my gaze from the *Vitis* hanging in tatters when, just hours before, it had danced over the tree and promised me a blaze of autumn colour.

Vitis coignetiae.

I do trade with my neighbours that tolerate the spill. The evergreen *Rosa* 'Cooperi' on the fence at the end serves us both, and there is give and take with the *Hedera colchica* that scrambles over the garage roofs. In the spring, its lush green foliage is a shiny contrast to the velvety foliage of the *Parthenocissus henryana*.

Choosing the position for your climbers also needs to be tailored to their requirements. Most are happy to have their feet in the shade, for this is where their seedlings will have originated, dropped by a bird or from the parent high above them. But sun is what they are after, and though *Lonicera*, *Holboellia* and some of the clematis will flower sufficiently in the shade, if they know they can get into the sun, they will be up and over the fence, leaving you with bare ankles to contend with if that is where the sun is to be found. That said, bare ankles come with the territory and can be avoided by careful training early in life and early in the season where the clematis are concerned. A sunny position will help to keep growth low down, and this is the reason that the *Trachelospermum* are clothed to the base on the south-facing fence. Grow them where they have to make an effort to reach the light and they will jettison lower limbs once they have what they need. I wish I had extended them the length of the fence in this position, as they have clothed themselves so effectively that they might as well be a hedge.

Clematis x *triternata* 'Rubromarginata'.

I have deliberately avoided climbers with showy flowers on the fences because I do not want to draw attention to the boundaries. Small-flowered *Clematis viticella* and *C.* x *triternata* 'Rubromarginata' clamber up the hot fences. The dark-flowered *Campsis* x *tagliabuana* 'Madame Galen' makes it through the clematis now but it has been a battle, as the clematis are fast in the spring and overwhelm the slow-to-wake trumpet vine. It is a case of early-season management, but the two are well matched today, now that the *Campsis* is maturing and has the stamina. I get away with growing a tangle of *Solanum laxum* 'Album' and evergreen *Holboellia* on the north-facing fence because both are tolerant of a little cool. *Holboellia latifolia* is a plant that is new to me in this garden, but I like it very much. It is a constant presence, its finely fingered palmate foliage is never dreary and its scented flowers are all pervading in April.

Campsis x *tagliabuana* 'Madame Galen'.

Annual and perennial climbers are also used to weave colour into the beds. *Ipomaea lobata* self-seeds in a hot summer, but I grow a few plants for the pots to add height and interest. While the coyote willows were with us, I grew a dark-flowered morning glory into their limbs. Even though the *Ipomoea* was an annual, it was tenacious and it was important to wait until the willows were strong enough or one would have been ruined by the other. Of all the plants in the garden, the climbers present perhaps the greatest management challenge, but it is a challenge worth taking on. The ugliness of the extension is softened, the garden ascends to the fourth-floor windows and appears to have no end, and my boundaries are clothed, even though they are sometimes straining at the seams.

Autumn

228

Persicaria

I have four varieties of *Persicaria* in the garden and I will always depend upon them. Some are big plants, but there is nothing wrong with putting big things into a small space – they add an air of excitement. Provided that the soil is reasonably retentive, they are easy plants and adapt to a range of conditions, being equally happy in a little shade as out in the sun. As foliage plants, they make a handsome foil for the first part of the summer, but several are key in providing colour when many plants are beginning to flounder in August. This is a critical time, caught in a hiatus when the garden is regrouping after the early push. Things can often look exhausted while the next wave of autumn performers is mustering, which is why the grasses, the aconites and verbena are useful in filling the gap. The late-flowering *Persicaria* are a mainstay of this season and will still be with us and looking good with the last of the dahlias.

Persicaria polymorpha.

You need to think carefully about the bistorts, for they make their presence felt over the course of the growing season. The American landscape designer Wolfgang Oehme introduced me to *Persicaria polymorpha* in Washington state about fifteen years ago. He was excited to have found it and was using it as a signature plant among drifts of lower perennials. Since then, it has become widely used here, though it is a big thing and not to everyone's taste. The new shoots have an alarming similarity to Japanese knotweed and look like they are going to be as far-reaching, but the plant is thoroughly clump-forming and well behaved in that respect. Growth masses to reach two metres high

PAGE 228
Persicaria amplexicaulis 'Alba'.

and as much across when established, but I keep it from sprawling by staking with hoops. The hellebores are happy in the shade it casts, and the late-flowering *Tricyrtis formosana* make their presence felt at its base and cover for the fact that this *Persicaria* is one of the earliest to flower. The flowers, which are cream, are grouped in triangular sprays at the end of each limb, like a giant *Aruncus*, and they are at their best for about a month from the end of June. They fade to brown, which I rather like, but you need to accept that they will alter the tone of the area in the process.

Tricyrtis formosana.

Conveniently, this is just about the point at which *Persicaria amplexicaulis* comes into its own. The long, heart-shaped foliage has been gathering strength until this point and forming a successful ground cover where it is grouped tightly. I grow the white form 'Alba' under the branches of the *Hydrangea aspera* 'Macrophylla', and the fine vertical spires of flower are thrown into relief by the shade. It is teamed here with the off-white *Actaea cordifolia* (which also scores a thicker vertical line), ink-blue *Aconitum* 'Spark's Variety' and *Ageratina altissima* (*Eupatorium rugosum* 'Braunlaub'). *Persicaria amplexicaulis* 'Rosea' is a pale, shell-pink form, which I do not grow here because it is inclined to be just a little too pretty, but I do have 'Firetail' near the *Rosa* × *odorata* 'Mutabilis'. They are the brightest of the red-flowered *Persicaria amplexicaulis* and will still be in flower in November. The insects love them.

Persicaria can last for years without division, but in restricted conditions such as these, I find that I have to remove a number of the slowly creeping rhizomes each spring to keep them within bounds. After seven years or so, the central clump is in need of division and this is best done as soon as growth is stirring. *Persicaria virginiana* var. *filiformis* has its own set of rules, however, and has become quite a prolific seeder in the shady parts at the end of the garden. It is one of the best late-foliage plants in the garden. The oval leaves are emerald-green, marked with a deep red chevron slash, like war paint.

Persicaria amplexicaulis 'Firetail'.

Though perfectly hardy, it is slow into action in the spring and needs warmth to get it going. I have tried it with some success in sunshine, but it colours a shrill, brilliant green in higher light levels. I prefer the depth of green that it retains in a little shade. Nestling close to the *Molinia caerulea* subsp. *arundinacea* 'Transparent' and either side of the path to the compost heap, it forms a low mound that is tall enough to wet your trousers to the knee when pushing past in the autumn. The tiny flowers open in late September, sent up on wire-thin stems to waist height. They are microscopic, no larger than pin-heads and, because the stems are almost black, all you are aware of is the fine gauzy lines of deep coral-pink extending above the mound mass of foliage. I originally teamed it up with the lime-leaved *Geranium* 'Ann Folkard', but it has slowly increased its range and is now finding the gaps elsewhere. Seedlings are left where they are in the shingle and pulled up a year later in early summer once they are in growth. At this point, they are easily moved and passed on to friends. Though they are slowly advancing here, the seedlings are easily weeded from the beds in spring and, so far, there have been no complaints of bad behaviour.

Planting Bulbs

It is always difficult to plan ahead and to put your head into another season but, of all the tasks in the autumn, bulb planting produces the most instant results. Bulbs are incredibly good value for the display that they yield, and planting them is lighting the blue touch paper for a more-or-less guaranteed awakening at the end of the winter. Unless I am purchasing expensive treasures or lilies for which there are only a certain number of suitable containers, I rarely purchase in small numbers. Buying wholesale is far cheaper than retail, and the bulbs arrive in their tens or, preferably, hundreds.

I always aim to write my bulb order in the spring because it is so easy to forget spring treasures by the time the bulb catalogues arrive in the summer. Though I never manage to do this, I concentrate my mind upon the gaps that I can see three seasons away. I make myself order as soon as the catalogues arrive so that I'm able to get the stock I want and there is still warmth in the ground to settle in the bulbs when they arrive.

The excitement of unpacking bulbs never dims, and they are immediately taken out of their boxes or bags to expose them to the air and prevent them from rotting. The garage is ideal as a holding place because it is cool and airy, but tubers and rhizomatous plants such as *Erythronium, Trillium, Lilium* and *Paris* are better stored in just-damp compost until you are ready to put them in their final position. *Cyclamen* are often offered as dry corms but they fail to establish well and are far better planted while in growth. *Cyclamen hederifolium* and *C. coum* have their own particular leaf markings, and spending time choosing your favourites is worth the effort if you can find containerized plants. I rarely plant *Galanthus* (snowdrops) as dormant bulbs because they take an age to establish once lifted and dried. Instead, they are moved in-the-green soon after they have flowered at the beginning of spring, and they grow into their new position before becoming dormant again, to give them a head start the following year.

Most of the bulbs are grown in pots and those that are planted in the ground are only put there once I know that a planting is settled. The early flux of spring bulbs is invaluable among the perennials, but once the bulbs are in the ground, it makes looking after a mixed planting that much more complex. Winter skeletons have to be removed, and mulch has to be in place before the bulbs are up. Here in London, where the winters are shorter, this brings the end of winter clear-up forward by a month. However, it is the bulbs that prevent the garden from being without interest early in the year and gradually they have found their way into the beds. Now that the beds are full to brimming, I have to do my very best to remember where I have put them. There are few things more disturbing than spearing a dormant bulb with your fork or hearing the crunch underfoot of a forgotten lily ready to emerge just below the surface.

I will empty the summer bedding and the basil as it declines to free up the pots for the bulbs that will be containerized. Each year I trial something new and, along with the favourites, there is a new list of bulbs that I want to get to know. Those favourites that were stored dry in the garage are brought out and cleaned in preparation. *Narcissus*, *Crocus* and *Iris* are potted up first, but the tulips can wait until November and are held back until the last of the annuals have had their day. The bulbs are planted close (but not so close that they are touching) for a good display and at about two-and-a-half to three times their own depth. After the pots are put into a protected corner, they are immediately covered with fleece or netting to keep the squirrels from digging them up. Squirrels are the worst pests there are until the bulbs have broken ground later in the winter. Several of the shorter-growing bulbs that are selected for the pans are brought up close to the house, but in the meantime they are tucked away in the frame. New lilies are set into a layer of sharp grit to help keep the ground slugs at bay.

Those bulbs that go directly into the garden are held back until late October when the planting is beginning to fall apart. Weaving my way into the beds on hands and knees is a fiddle and, if I had a larger garden, I would simply cut the perennials back at this point to make the bulb planting easier. The reason that I make it difficult for myself is that I like to leave as much winter interest as possible – the skeletons are good for a while yet and preferable to naked and unprotected soil.

PAGE 233
Late-flowering *Hedychium gardnerianum*.

PAGES 234–5
Persicaria virginiana var. *filiformis* and *Molinia caerulea* subsp. *arundinacea* 'Transparent'.

PAGES 236–7
Saving seed from *Stipa barbata*.

PAGES 238–9
Early autumn, with *Melianthus major* in the foreground and a new injection of colour from *Nerine bowdenii*.

Harvest

A new mood replaces the rush that has guided us into August. The sun is already tilting so that the shadow from the house is noticeably longer in the mornings, but the beds are as full as they ever will be. It takes careful planning for the garden still to be looking good by this stage, and the gentle disorder that you see here now could equally be one of chaos. The inky flowered *Veratrum nigrum* would be leaning into their neighbours had they not been staked when they were still just knee-high, and the tomatoes would be a riot of limbs had they not been pinched out to focus their resources. Likewise, the *Tagetes* would nearly be over if I had not kept them deadheaded. The truth of the matter is that this is the season of ripening and maturation, the plant world's insurance policy that it will continue into another year.

The relaxed atmosphere that comes with this end-of-the-holidays feeling can easily engender a false sense of security, but it is important to maintain control so that the garden continues to produce. The 'Bengal Crimson' roses will muster another crop of flowers, if not two, before the year is out if the spent heads are removed before they try to form hips. I also fool the *Tagetes* into flower by deadheading and thereby goading them on. There is no reason for the dahlias not to carry us handsomely into the autumn, and picking for the house is the best way to keep them in good condition. I never let a bud mature on the plant and I remove it halfway to opening, cutting the flowers to a strong new shoot to make room for a further succession of blooms. This regular attention not only keeps the kitchen table colourful, but also maintains the plants in best condition – in a good year, the dahlias are often some of the best plants in the garden in October.

In the vegetable beds and on the allotment, the production line has been running since early May with cut-and-come-again salad and herbs, but a blind eye turned now and the courgettes will run to marrows in less than a week. Keeping up with what is produced by the vegetable beds is important in terms of deceiving the vegetables into continued production. A marrow is the endgame for a courgette, so remove it while it is still young and the plant will replenish itself. The same goes for the climbing French beans, and it is important to keep picking regularly so that they continue to flower while the growing season is with us and, in turn, continue to produce. Young vegetables are one of the luxuries of growing your own, and for a good six weeks it is a daily task to keep on top of the production line.

PAGE 240
Tomato 'Gardener's Delight' and 'Sungold' climb the fence at the end of the garden.

Most years will produce an excess of something. A cool season will see the chard, the Russian kale and the parsley flourish; a warm, dry summer, the borlotti beans and the basil. Basil is useless in this climate if it doesn't get the heat it needs – when I grew it in the open ground, I had to make do with a pinch or a mere garnish if the year wasn't with me. The frame allows the opportunity of excess and, when that happens, it is good to have a plan in place to avoid the feeling of wastefulness. I will pinch out all the tips on the basil to promote a new crop of foliage and make them into pesto. We do the same with the sage, rocket and also with the sorrel, transforming a considerable bulk of leaf into intense pots of garnish. The pesto will keep for a month to six weeks in the fridge if you make sure that there is always a skim of olive oil over the surface.

I could never have too many tomatoes, and they are one of the reasons that I pine for a glasshouse. The smell of them growing evokes memories of my Grandpa's vegetable garden. Their ease and responsiveness provide such instant gratification, and I have only ever been unlucky enough to lose one crop to blight. This happened in the wet summer of 2007 and it was one of the reasons that I decided to take on an allotment so that I could rest the beds in the garden. Harvesting the tomatoes is as good as picking any fruit, and many of them don't make it into the house, as they never taste better than with the warmth of the sun still in them. Though I always try something new, 'Gardener's Delight' and 'Sungold' remain my favourites. I will pick them daily, gathering the fruit in the afternoon rather than the morning so that the fruit is warm and tastier for it. Picking regularly ensures that I catch those that have split before they start to rot.

As we move into September and the sun dips away still further, I remove a portion of the foliage so that the light gets to the fruit to ripen them. Chill mornings bring dew and with dampness the increased risk of botrytis, so the light and the air are important. If we have an Indian summer, the remaining trusses will ripen on the plant, but if not, they are harvested whole and put in the garage where they continue to ripen. The remains of the potatoes are dug and bagged before the slugs get to them. The courgettes that have turned to marrows are put on the street so that neighbours can take them, and I pick over the kale and the broccoli for cabbage white butterflies so that, beyond this bountiful time, there is plenty to look forward to.

Seed-Saving

Saving seed has become a habit – there is something compelling about having all that potential locked up and waiting and sitting in the palm of your hand. I harvest what must be a tiny proportion of what is actually produced because, every year, a multitude of seed finds its way back into the system to take its chances with the wet winters, the slugs and the riot of other plants competing for the same piece of ground. The majority of plants are left to seed and I do not curtail the cycle by deadheading where it is not needed. Short-lived perennials such as *Knautia macedonica*, *Gaura lindheimeri* and *Erigeron karvinskianus* find their way to the position that suits them most, and there is nothing quite like a plant that has arrived on its own for getting its roots down and thriving. I also like the seed heads, the hips and the fruits, and the birds like them, too, often feeding here in a frenzy as a particular plant ripens.

Gathering the seed of *Papaver somniferum*.

The annuals are entirely dependent upon seed as a method of reproduction. I like to have them in the garden because they rarely appear in the same place more than once and they keep the planting from feeling static. The black opium poppies are a good example – they were scattered where I needed some immediate impact in the early days while everything was still small. They continue to find a niche where the ground is disturbed, along with the *Eschscholzia californica* and the lime-leaved nasturtium 'Mahogany', and are useful in this respect because they give the garden a lived-in feeling. The half-hardy annuals are also harvested so that I can be independent the following spring, and the *Cleome hassleriana* (syn. *spinosa*) 'Violet Queen', the *Nicotiana* and the *Ipomoea* are watched carefully so that I can get my share of their seeds before they drop.

Nasturtium 'Mahogany'.

Seed is easy to harvest if you keep your eyes tuned to the ripening process, and it is important to wait until the seed is mature before removing it from the plant. Some is easier to gather than most. Lift the raft of foliage where the nasturtiums trail along the ground and there will be freshly deposited seed already broken free and waiting. The poppies are ready when the apertures at the top of the pepper pot open, while the silky vapour trails of the *Stipa barbata* detach when they are ripe and land like darts in the ground. The awns twist to earth with the wind, detaching when the seed is drilled home. The seed is easy to gather and, as this *Stipa* is from highland steppe, it is better germinated in a pot in the comparative dry of the frame.

Geranium and some of the *Euphorbia* fling their seed to distribute it far and wide, making it almost impossible to get to it at just the right moment. Seed becomes ripe one day and is dispersed the next. However, a paper bag or a stocking placed over the seed head once it starts to brown will catch it. Where seed is tiny or a fiddle to pick, I harvest the whole seed head and place it upside down in a bowl in the garage to dry.

When storing seed, it is important that it is dry because it can easily rot if you are harvesting in a wet year or towards the end of the season. I place the seed capsules on newspaper and work the seed free from the casing once it is dry. The seed is separated from the chaff by folding the paper in half and tapping the ravine of seed with the flick of your thumb. After the seed has worked its way to the top of the crease, it can easily be separated from the chaff. It is then put in an envelope, labelled and stored in Tupperware in the fridge or a cool corner, as it has a sell-by date and degrades faster in warmer temperatures.

The in-built senescence is not uniform and some seeds last longer than others. Legumes can be stored for years, while the seeds of the umbelliferous plants and the buttercup family have a short life span – they become infertile if you keep them over the winter. This is why I sow the *Bupleurum*, hellebores, *Aquilegia* and peonies immediately they ripen. I like the harvest of the marble-sized seed of the *Paeonia delavayi* as they drop heavily into the palm of your hand, and there is usually a pot of them germinating in the cold frame. Come the spring, I will be grateful for having taken my own share out of the life cycle, as there is nothing quite like the feeling of new life at your fingertips.

Late-Flowering Bulbs

In the middle of September, if I am lucky, the *Amaryllis belladonna* stirs from dormancy. They are going against the flow at this point, with the garden showing signs of falling away into autumn, but they are always welcome when they do decide to send up their flowers. The stems are mahogany-red and push up strongly with three to five buds per stem. They are bait for slugs after the heavy dews and, as the flowers are fleeting, it is worth steeling your conscience and destroying the slugs to preserve their purity. Though some forms are rosy, mine is pearly, shaded pink from the tips to a throat that is almost white. They are always out with the *Datura metaloides* and the webs of autumn spiders.

The *Amaryllis* flower erratically here, the show being entirely dependent upon the heat of the preceding summer. This is a plant that needs to bake, and the hot spots are rarely hot enough, given the amount of growth that happens around them. In their homeland of

Amaryllis belladonna.

South Africa, and in California where they have naturalized, *Amaryllis belladonna* grow on rocky hillsides where the drainage is sharp and the baking sun ripens the bulb. Though hardy in most of Britain, provided it has a choice location, the best plants I have ever seen here are those on the Scilly Isles, where the bulbs work their way to the surface in the sandy ground. The extra light and warmth promote an exuberant display that puts mine to shame.

Nevertheless, I do feel a small triumph in the years that they flower, and I grow them on their own at the end of the herb bed, which is the best I can offer in terms of a south-facing position. The foliage is up early in spring and feeds the bulb until it withers away in July, but it isn't up for long enough before the rest of the garden around them is mustering. The *Colchicum*, on the other hand, have been in leaf and feeding for the best part of the winter and are gone by the time the riot in the garden is in full swing and shading them out. I have always enjoyed *Colchicum* leafage in winter because, as long as you can keep it slug-free, it is lustrous, light-reflecting and verdant at the dullest time of the year. The problem of its disappearance is resolved if it is partnered correctly with plants that emerge later in the season and cover for the gaps they leave. The naked flowers look wonderful among a net of prostrate *Aster divaricatus* or frothing *Erigeron karvinskianus*.

Also from South Africa are the *Eucomis*, *Crinum* and *Nerine*. *Eucomis comosa* 'Sparkling Burgundy' has been good since it emerged in the spring, and the long, strap-shaped foliage is aptly named. I first saw it in Seattle where it was twice the size and glistening with health. I learned there that it takes easily from leaf cuttings and this is how I have developed the clump that sits among the coppery *Thamnochortus insignis*. The elongated inflorescence is a curious fruity pink, and it comes as the deeply rooting *Crinum* x *powellii* 'Album' are fading at the front. These late-flowering bulbs are indispensable for their ability to refresh a garden that can easily look exhausted.

The *Nerine bowdenii* were originally given to me by my great friend Geraldine, who had them growing in not much more than rubble at the base of a south-facing wall. High up on the wall was a fig that fruited well, but it did not shade the base where Geraldine had them teamed with Algerian iris. Autumn-flowering bulbs have a short season of dormancy and should be moved or planted as soon as they become dormant. As they start into growth again in late August, you have to order early or seize the moment and move them as soon as the foliage withers. Unfortunately, in the case of the *Nerine*, this is in late summer, not long before you start to see the first signs of flower.

Crinum x *powellii* 'Album'.

Eucomis comosa 'Sparkling Burgundy'.

The *Nerine* are happiest when the bulbs are congested, and they like to live in one place without disturbance. They sit on top of the ground in a cluster, but they are rarely so dormant that they give up their purchase with ease and you have to prise a clump of bulbs away from the parent group. They take a couple of years to settle down after splitting and are nothing more than leaf until they are ready to flower. During this time you have to exercise patience.

The flowers start to show signs of life in mid-September as the foliage begins to wither. The sheath holding the buds is like a taper, rising to roughly knee height when the bulbs are naked. At the beginning of October, the papery casing is cast aside and the buds are revealed in a cluster of eight or nine. They open in sequence as they expand, wavy edged and held on spokes that radiate into a half-dome. The flowers are unashamedly pink, the colour of bubble gum or artificially coloured sweets. At this time of year, as the light declines, they are extraordinary in their intensity. The lime-green of the nasturtium foliage is at its most vivid then, and the first of the autumn colour is joining the riot, pushing the boundaries of the colour palette further than you might consider feasible at any other time of the year.

I have increased the *Nerine* slowly over the years so that there is now a line of them following the edge of the path, tracing the position of the celandines, which are currently dormant. While the *Colchicum* and the *Amaryllis* flower for a week or ten days at most, the *Nerine* are still there in late November. Unlike many of my treasures, they are plentiful enough to be picked for the house, combined with the last of the dahlias. When the frost hits, they are still going strong, even when the garden is browning and thinning around them.

Nerine bowdenii with the seed heads of *Dierama pulcherrimum.*

Propagation

I find it hard not to propagate my own plants, even though the garden is brimful and there is little space for anything new. I do this every year with seed, division and cuttings, and there is always excess as a result. Learning the art of restraint is a difficult thing when it is easy to multiply. Whether it is your own material or seeds and cuttings purloined or given to you with gardener's generosity, there is always the consequence of something in the frame that needs a home. The knock-on effect is 'the corner of shame', which develops once the plants outgrow the needs of the frame. Without fail, these orphans provoke guilt.

Right now, to illustrate my point, there are two balsam poplars straining in pots when they desperately want to be trees. The branches, from a tree I know in the country, were brought into the house so that I could enjoy the musky perfume of the leaves. Their unfurling foliage has a hauntingly delicious scent, which, for me, is the personification of bud burst, but they rooted in the jug during the time they were scenting the kitchen. Their lust for life could not go without reward. They were potted up and, though I gave the bulk away to friends and clients with rolling acres, I kept two back in the hope that one day a suitable home, to which I would have easy access, would suggest itself. The *Euonymus planipes*, which I took as seed from a shrub in the Netherlands, need to get their feet in the ground, as do the winter honeysuckles that are just too big to work into the planting here. There are a host of hellebore seedlings and countless others that have to prove their worth and flower before they earn a home. Young plants were always made with good intentions, but finding a home for them is not always easy.

The propagation year has its seasons but I like to think of it as starting in autumn. Seed of hardy plants, harvested over the summer, is nearly always better in the ground than sitting in an envelope and degrading in Tupperware. Some seed is only short-lived and will rarely develop if you keep it over the winter to sow in the spring, while others need the winter to break dormancy. The seed of the hellebores is the first to ripen and, where I have a form that I particularly like, I keep a vigil as the pods begin to lose their colour so that the seed is not lost when it drops.

The seed is spread evenly over a pot and separated so that it doesn't touch. This is easy with 'handleable' seed but it is worth mastering how to distribute a pinch if the seed is fine. You will always be spreading more than you think, and one of the perils of being a young seedling is overcrowding after germination because they are more prone to rotting off if they are cheek by jowl and straining. You want to be able to leave seedlings in situ at least until they have their first set of adult foliage, which is a year minimum for hellebores, peonies and most trees and shrubs. The seed is put in a clay pot because clay breathes, and a fine layer of grit is spread over the top, just enough to put the seed into darkness. I prefer this to covering with compost, as the grit is inert and it keeps the slugs at bay should they be tempted. The newly sown pots are then covered with netting or glass, to protect them from birds and squirrels, and put in the cool down by the compost heap. When autumn comes and the frame is stripped of basil, they are moved into the protection so that they don't lie wet in the winter.

There are two seasons for dividing the perennials and I use both where it is appropriate. An early start in September is the ideal because the new divisions will have time to settle in soil warmed by the summer and dampened by autumn weather. The second season is in early spring when there is movement in the young shoots and time enough for them to settle before summer kicks in. Though most perennials aren't too fussy about whether they are divided in autumn or spring, grasses need spring division, as their dormancy is clearly defined in the winter. Root growth of most plants happens in all but the coldest weather, even if they appear to be dormant above ground, but grasses will sit in shock and be prone to rotting if divided at the wrong time. The same can be said of bamboos, which makes perfect sense once you think of them as a giant perennial.

Regular division is not a necessity, and long-lived plants like peony, *Trillium* and day lily can go for decades without it, but the pioneer species that spread out fast from the central crown will need it once they start to lose vigour. The likes of bergamot and creeping asters will require division every third or fourth year, *Persicaria* and Siberian iris every sixth or seventh. It is a simple exercise that involves lifting the whole clump and prising apart the most vigorous shoots at the perimeter. Though not always easy to do, the core of the original plant should be discarded. All I have to do is look at the corner of shame to know that this is the only way forward.

Revitalizing the soil before replanting is fundamental to a good start. I am always grateful to the compost heap for providing such an endless source of goodness at this point, and I cannot help but think that the parents of these new slips have contributed to it along the way. A handful of blood fish and bone is scattered over a square metre and worked in, too, and I'll water in to settle the soil around the young roots.

As soon as the trees and shrubs lose their foliage, I take hardwood cuttings. The sap is still in the wood at this point, which will promote roots over the winter and spring. Though willows and poplars can be struck at almost any time in the year, the success rate will drop away with most woody plants once you have reached the end of the year and the sap is drawn back into the roots. Though I don't need to, I take a batch of vine cuttings every autumn, and the strawberry grape has made its way into many a client's garden as a result. Roses, woody *Lonicera*, *Cornus* and *Sambucus* also respond well. Pencil-thick wood is the ideal, with a horizontal cut immediately below the bottom bud. The cutting should be about the same length as a pencil, too, with a sloping cut immediately above the top bud.

Hardwood cuttings of *Vitis* 'Fragola'.

PAGE 249
Splitting *Iris* x *robusta* 'Gerald Darby'.

PAGES 250–1
The *Brugmansia arborea* rallies with a late flush of flowers.

PAGES 252–3
The deck is gradually covered with a blanket of fallen hornbeam leaves.

PAGES 254–5
The Virginia creeper, dahlias and *Tricyrtis* at the end of the garden.

We were told at horticultural college that this was to shed the water in the winter but I find it helps to tell bottom and top when you plunge them half their length into a 50:50 compost of loam and sharp grit. They will be found a winter home in the frame and be rooted by spring.

Sarcococca, box, camellias, bay and myrtle are easily rooted from autumn cuttings but I'll wait until spring to take cuttings of the silvery Mediterranean plants if I need them to replace a plant that looks like it is on its last legs. I am slowly learning to take only what I need but old habits are often hard to kick and the corner of shame lives on.

Changes

With each year that passes, I grow to like the autumn more. It is a big season where transformation is rapid and change is all-embracing. You cannot help but look up and out to take in your surroundings. In the city, this is important because a season can so easily come and go without you noticing the finer detail. We do not have the reference of big skies or hedgerow or woodland to show us the subtlety of the season's shift, but our gardens, parks and street trees help us to be part of something that's bigger. In all but the most built-up areas, the city smells different – of vegetation and leaf-litter – and, for a few weeks, the pavements are eclipsed by fallen foliage as if the forest had come to town.

Cercis canadensis 'Forest Pansy'.

Just six months ago, on the other side of the year, the other big season, spring, arrived in a frenzy but, now that the growing has happened, the overwhelming feeling is one of letting go. I do exactly that once I know that the balance has tipped and that there's no point in putting up a fight to keep the garden together. It is time to submit and it usually happens when the *Nerine* paint their gash of pink along the path. The first of the colour is beginning to show in the vegetation that surrounds us, and the *Parthenocissus quinqefolia* that creeps through from next door is the first to colour scarlet. It is almost exactly the same shade as the dahlias at the end.

The Virginia creeper colours early and is made all the more intense by the unchanged greenery around it, but soon the rest of the garden begins to shift, flashing occasional leaf colour and gathering apace towards a climax at the end of October. If I had more space, I would plant specifically for this season, with stands of deciduous *Euonymus*, maple and birch. I would have hip-bearing roses, fruiting hawthorns and crab apples, flaring brightly before dropping away to the monochrome of winter. I would plan for autumn on a big scale to distract me for a change from the detail.

PAGE 256
Vitis coignetiae.

I have embraced the season here in the garden as best I can where space is at a premium. The trees are key because they provide a backdrop, and I have ensured that they are well paced and enduring. The *Liquidambar styraciflua* on the pavement at the front of the house is often in colour for the best part of eight weeks and, during that time, the tree changes like a fire that is at first taking, then burning hard before going out. Colour first appears in late September, with occasional leaves turning amber and maroon-red, but it peaks in early November to fill the front windows with a blaze of colour. Whereas many trees colour for a moment in a season that is often beset by rain-laden winds, the *Liqudambar* is particular in its ability to hang on to foliage, which continues through to the end of November. The range of colour is important and it heightens the depth of the experience, with the foliage moving from oxblood and crimson through saffron to pale primrose.

The hornbeam provides the change in the body of the garden, colouring up at the height of the season. Until now it has provided a simple, uncomplicated backdrop, but it changes in volume when it blazes yellow and your eye is drawn to it immediately. When you stand close, there is a golden glow that bathes everything around it, like a buttercup held under your chin. It does not last long, two to three weeks in a benign autumn, but when the foliage has dropped, the skirt of fallen leaves on the ground continues to bounce colour upward. The skirt takes a while to brown and I leave it where it is until it begins to lie wet and loses its vibrancy.

The sun slides into the garden from an ever-increasing angle and hits the *Cornus kousa* full on. Its leaves shift from a curious reddish-brown to a bright candy-pink streaked with yellow, which came as a surprise when it first happened and took me a while to like. Of all the seasons, autumn is the one when you have to let go and just enjoy the contrast because there are always surprises thrown together and one year is never the same as the next. The *Vitis coignetiae*, which I thought I had contained on the garage wall, will suddenly be visible in the neighbour's beech tree and, when it colours up, it is all too obvious that it has escaped my garden. The leaves are the size of dinner plates, veined with amber and yellow over deep maroon midribs. As it grows in the shade, it rarely colours red like the one in the sun used to, climbing through the hornbeam.

The *Cercis canadensis* 'Forest Pansy' is the star of the season and set up to be so, framed as it is within the picture window of the basement. Over the years, I have allowed it to lean to one side and have pruned it in a Zen-like exercise so that it remains within bounds. For the

Cornus kousa var. *chinensis*.

summer, the foliage has been rich and dark, lighting up in the evening when the sun streams through it, but it colours brilliantly come the autumn. Carmine-pink, amber, scarlet and tangerine appear over the course of a month, and I pray for a still month so that we can enjoy the colour that is reflected into the house. The water bowl gets filled with the fallen foliage, and the deck is covered for a month, when it is perfectly acceptable to let go of the reins and just watch it all happen.

Preparing for Winter

Towards the end of October, I begin to keep a beady eye on the weather. Though rare here in London, and we often escape for another month at least, frost is in the air, and cold nights and wet in combination are not good for many of the more tender plants.

As if in a perverse countermovement, the *Brugmansia* is always at its best now, reserving the greater majority of its flowers until the weather cools. There are too many blooms to count and, on a still, chill autumn evening, the whole of the end of the garden is shrouded in their perfume.

I have had the mother plant now for the best part of eighteen years. The ritual of bringing it inside marks an annual turning point when the summer display of pots is replaced with plants that appear on the other side of winter. I leave it for as long as possible, so that I can enjoy the last of the display, as many of the plants look almost better now than they ever have. This is an anxiety-inducing process, which in the past has led to late-night trips down the garden to throw fleece over the limbs of the *Brugmansia*. Some years I have escaped the first few ticklings of frost this way, but you have to respect realities if you want to push the boundaries of hardiness. The freeze will do for the nasturtiums, which are the litmus test, and I know when they collapse that action must be taken if I am not to lose my tender perennials.

When I arrived here, and in the spirit of experimentation, I tested the microclimate by planting the *Brugmansia* in the most sheltered corner in the angle of the house. I had seen mature plants in Auckland that were tree-like in proportion and had a fantasy that I might be able to walk under the branches one day if the plant were able to weather the first few winters. In general, with plants of borderline hardiness, the older they are, the more resilient they will be to cold, but the mother plant was cut to the ground by frost, even though its lower limbs were encased in bubble wrap. The base of the plant and the roots, which had been protected from the freeze, came back in early

Brugmansia arborea.

Pelargonium moved into the shelter of the garage for protection against the winter weather.

summer, but the summer wasn't long enough to generate sufficient growth to risk the experiment a second year running, so I dug it up and it has remained in a pot ever since.

Though the stems are twisted and thickened by age, the plant is restricted now by the size of the pot. This is the largest camellia pot I could find and it has just enough depth of soil to prevent it from drying out more than once a day in hot weather. After a summer's growth, it reaches nearly three metres across and almost as high, and it is impossible to move it more than a short distance.

I have learned through necessity that drastic action can be tolerated, and the only way to move the *Brugmansia* to its winter quarters is to prune and decant it so that it is manageable. The limbs are reduced back into the old wood to a framework that allows me to fit it into the garage. The oldest wood is often rapidly replaced with strong new shoots, and a clean cut made immediately above an outward-facing leaf joint means that it can easily rebranch in the right direction. When the plant was put into the camellia pot earlier in the summer, I laid a rope under the root ball so that it could easily be pulled from the pot after gently pushing the pot onto its side. I lie on my back with the rope in my hands and my feet pushing against the rim of the pot until the congested root ball comes free. The root ball is then reduced with an old pruning saw to a size that can fit into a pot that I am able to carry to the garage. Here, it is repotted into good compost and kept just moist. The top light from the Perspex garage roof is enough to keep the plant going. It loves this cool winter living and is in full leaf again and producing the first of many flowers by April.

Salvia discolor.

To date, I have got away with bringing the *Salvia discolor*, pineapple sage and the lemon verbena up to the house where they have survived the cold. Once again, they are left on the dry side, as are the plants in the frame. Bubble wrap helps to keep this frost-free, but in a thorough freeze I bring the *Pelargonium* cuttings inside, to be sure. I must admit to leaving the *Fuchsia* 'Thalia' as sacrifice to the frost, since they always do better from young plants potted up in spring. The *Pelargonium* cuttings are happy to be kept on the dry side in the garage, but the fuchsias hate it, so I treat myself to new plants from the local nursery.

Frosted *Fuchsia* 'Thalia'.

Dahlias, cannas and the hardy gingers are left in the ground rather than lifting and storing them inside. Even in the coldest of winters here in Peckham, the frost never gets far enough into the ground to damage their tubers. For safety, during the first few years here, I mulched them along with the *Melianthus* but I don't bother with that now – much the bigger problem in winter is ground slugs. After about three or four years, the dahlias need to be dug up, divided and given a new lease of life if they are not to dwindle away to nothing.

The remaining tender perennials are brought close to the house and tidied up on the terrace. The begonias will have been reduced to nothing at the first hint of frost aond it is important to bring them inside because their corms are tender. These are left dry in the pots until March, when they are repotted and kept just moist to get them restarted. The parent *Pelargonium* are moved down to the shelter of the terrace. I keep cuttings going in the frame. These are my fall-back, but the old plants have character and I like the gangly limbs and swollen knuckles. The bamboo hedge shelters them and keeps them on the dry side, which is key to their survival because they hate nothing more than the combination of cold and wet. They often stay there well into January, as long as there are no prolonged freezes, but, generally, they are happier in the garage. The space inside is limited and they have to be bundled together like commuters on a train. They strain for light and lose a good percentage of their growth, but they can deal with a little drought and are easy to keep in a state of semi-dormancy over the winter.

In reality, the garden draws back into itself for just the briefest of periods, and there are already signs of the coming season on ripened wood – cinnamon buds on the *Hamamelis* and a constellation of tiny flower buds already formed on the *Cornus*. The shiny filigree foliage of *Ferula tingitana* 'Cedric Morris' is already up in the wreckage of the cannas and, as if to signal that all is not lost, there are the first November flowers on the Algerian iris. This is a garden that will demand less for the next few weeks but it will continue to delight while it is resting.

Index
Figures in italics indicate illustrations

Acanthus mollis 'Hollard's Gold' 75, *75*

Achillea 91

Aconitum 'Sparks Variety' 112, 124, 230

Actaea (*Cimicifuga*) 122, 142, 230

Adiantum venustum 143, *143*

Ageratina altissima 124, 142, 230

Alcea rugosa 108, 184, *190–1*, 193, *214–15*

Allium 157, 194

    A. hollandicum 58, 137, *150–1*

    A. stipitatum 'Mount Everest' 138

    A. triquetrum 34, 196

Amaryllis belladonna 170, 244–5, *244*, 246

Amelanchier 38

Anemanthele lessoniana 178

Anemone nemorosa *138*, 139

Aquilegia 'Yellow Star' 138, 157, 194, *194*, 244

Arisaema 62, 139

Arum italicum 'Marmoratum' *68–9*, 72, 75

Asarum europaeum 93, 143, *143*

Astelia chathamica 142

asters 197, 245, 248

Astrantia 'Hadspen Blood' *176*

Athyrium 'Ghost' 144, *144*

autumn *28–31*, *42–3*, 224–63

    changes 257–9

    harvest 240–2

    late-flowering bulbs 244–6

    Persicaria 229–31

    planting spring bulbs 231–2

    propagation 246–9, 257

    seed-saving 243–4, 247

bamboo 64, 73–4, 159–60, 169, 197

    light effect 112, 159–60, 199

    planting/dividing 61, 169, 248

    wind effect 23, 35, *159*

Baptisia australis 171

bare-root plants, planting 61

begonias 158–9, 261

Betula albosinensis 38–9

Bidens ferulifolia *176*, 184, *214–15*

birds 178, 196, 198, 222, 243

Blechnum chilense 143

boundaries 62, 64, 196, 221–3

box 63–4, *63*, 140, *145*, 199, 257

Brugmansia arborea 78, 158, 197, *250–1*, 259–60, *259*

buddleia 19, 180, 196

bulbs

    late-flowering 244–6

    spring *46–7*, 90, 93, 109–11, 120–2, 158, 231–2

Bupleurum longifolium 193, 194, *194*, 244

Calamagrostis 58

calendulas 95

Campsis × *tagliabuana* 223, *223*

Canna 58, 178, *178*, 260

Carpinus see hornbeam

Catalpa × *erubescens* 'Purpurea' 39–40

celandines 95

Centaurea macrocephala 193

Cephalaria dipsacoides 58, 108, 217

Cercis

    C. canadensis 23, 26–7, 36, 62, *62*, 110, 121, *130–1*, 200, 257, *258–9*

Chappell, Peter 170

Chatto, Beth 59, 110, 127

Cimicifuga see Actaea

Clematis 80, 89, 137, 220, 222

    C. cirrhosa var. *purpurascens* 'Freckles' *68–9*, 75, *75*

    C. heracleifolia 'Cassandra' *56*

    C. viticella 80, 223

    C. × *triternata* 'Rubromarginata' 80, 178, 222, 223

Cleome hassleriana 56, 96, 159, 193, *216*, 217, 243

Clerodendrum bungei 19

climbers 220–3, 257

cloches 50, *148–9*, 153

Colchicum 245, 246

cold frame 50, 97, 109, 158

colour 112, 178, 183-4, 193, 199, *208-9*

compost 33-4, 60, 62, 96, *106*, 109, 158

compost heaps 22, 37, *44-5*, 58, 90, 248

Compton, Tania 99

Cornus kousa var. *chinensis* 'China Girl' 40, 248, 258, *258*, 261

Cosmos atrosanguineus 158-9, *201*

crimson glory vine 89

Crinum x *powellii* 74, 245, *245*

Crocosmia 'Lucifer' *66-7*, 121, 124, 178, 179, *179*, 184, *190-1*, 193

Crocus 94, 110, *116-17*, 232

cut flowers *68-9*, 154, 176-9

Cyclamen 19, 73, *73*, 74-5, 143, 231

Cytisus battandieri 19, 34, 36, 38-9, 98

dahlias 154, 229, 241, 246, *254-5*, 260-1

Daphne bholua 65, 76-7, *76*

Datura *210-11*, 244

day lilies *see Hemerocallis*

decks, wooden 36, *166-7*, 252-3

Dianthus carthusianorum 77, 193, *193*

Dicentra 92, 137, *137*, 139, 142, 144

Dierama 108, 170, 193, 202-3, 217, 246

Disporum 138, *138*

Dracunculus vulgaris 77

Dryopteris 139, 143, *143*

ecosystem 196-9

Epimedium 60, 64, 74, 93, 98, 126-8, *126-9*, 132-3

Erigeron karvinskianus 94, 243, 245

Eryngium 58, 199

E. *agavifolium* 123, 179-80, 202-3, *214-15*

E. *ebracteatum* 217

E. *giganteum* *41*, 107, 121, 193, 202-3

Erythronium 139, *139*, 231

Eschscholzia californica 92, 95, 243

eucalyptus 22, 34

Eucomis comosa 245, *245*

Euonymus planipes 247, 257

Eupatorium rugosum 'Braunlaub' 124, 142, 230

Euphorbia 137, 197, 243-4

E. *cornigera* 193

E. *dulcis* 'Chameleon' 108

E. *mellifera* 64, *64*, 141, 142, 182

evening primrose 109, 178, 184

evergreen plants 61, 62-4, 74, 75, 92-3

fences 34, 62

ferns 60, 74, 98, 127, 137, 139, 143-4

fertilizers 61, 248

Ferula tingitana 'Cedric Morris' 122, 140, 261

fleece 50

foliage 199

autumn 257-9

spring *134-5*, 140-4

Fritillaria 111, *111*, 181

front garden 64-75

frost damage *51*, 57, 259-61

fruit trees 34, 257

Fuchsia 19, 260, *260*

Galanthus (snowdrops) *86-7*, 97-100, *98-9*, 142, 177

dividing/planting 94, 231-2

G. 'S. Arnott' 74, 76, 99

Garrett, Fergus 218

Gaura lindheimeri 217, 243

Genista aetnensis 38, 74

Gentiana asclepiadea 139

Geranium 243-4

G. 'Anne Folkard' *188-9*, 193, 231

G. *macrorrhizum* 'White-Ness' 74, 93

G. 'Patricia' (Brempat) 92, 93, 112, *176*, *186-7*, *206-7*

Gillennia trifoliata 58, 123, 171, *171*

Gladiolus tristis 77-8, 140, *140*

grasses 58, 142, 200, 229
    division 248
    steppe-land/prairie 61, 200, 243
Great Dixter 78, 95, 141, 195, 218
ground cover 92–4
Gunnera 60

Hamamelis 78–80, 261
    H. mollis 79
    H. × *intermedia* 68–9, 78–9, *79*, 82–3
harvest 241–2
Hedera colchica 64, 221, *221*, 222
hedging 64, 159
Hedychium gardnerianum 233
Helenium 124
Helleborus 99–100, 197, 230, 244, 247
    H. hybridus 86–7, *88*, 99
    H. orientalis *98*, 100
    H. × *ericsmithii* 72, 74, 75
Hemerocallis (day lilies) 248
    H. altissima 78, 195
    H. citrina × *ochroleuca* 195, *195*
    H. dumortieri 194
    H. 'Hyperion' 195
    H. lilioasphodelus 142, 194, *194*
    H. 'Stafford' 93, 111, 178, 184, *190–2*, 193, 194–5
herbs 37, 144, 153, 241–2, 247, 260
Hinkley, Dan 138
Holboellia latifolia 77, 222, 223
holly 64, 141
hollyhocks 124, 180
Home Farm 18, 24, 33, 50, 169, 184, 194
honey fungus 34, 36, 39, 73
honeysuckle *see Lonicera*
hornbeam 32, 36, 39, 98, 112, *114–15*, 128, 140, 252–3, 258
Hydrangea
    H. aspera 57, 98, 180, 206–7, 230
    H. quercifolia 'Snow Queen' 74

Impatiens tinctoria 197
insects 58, 178–9, 197–9, 222
Ipomaea 96, 178, *178*, 218, 223, 243
Iris 169–71, 232
    Algerian 170, 245, 261
    I. chrysographes 58, 123, 142, 171, *171*
    I. foetidissima 169–70
    I. fulva *168*, 171
    I. histrioides 'Geroge' 110, *110*
    I. germanica 169
    I. japonica 'Ledger' *170*
    I. 'Katharine Hodgkin' 110
    I. lazica 170
    I. reticulata 109, 110, 170
    I. sibirica 171, 248
    I. unguicularis 74, *74*, 75, 170, 177
    I. × *robusta* 'Gerald Darby' 170–1, *170*, *249*
ivy 64, 141, 198, 221

jasmine 19, 77
jonquils 111, *137*

Knautia macedonica 243
knife, Turkish *48*, 50, 91

Lamium orvala 137–8
Lenten rose *see Helleborus*
light 112, 121, 184
lighting 35
Lilium 92, 180–3, 231, 232
    beetle 181, 182, 197
    L. 'African Queen' 77, *181*, 182
    L. 'Citronella' 183, *188–9*, 193
    L. 'Golden Splendor' Group 77
    L. henryi 123, 124, 178, 183, *183*, *190–1*
    L. pardalinum var. *giganteum* 182–3, *182*, *186–7*
    L. regale 77, 180–1, *180*, 182, 183
    L. speciosum 181, 182, *182*
lime tree 64, 73

Liquidambar styraciflua 73, 74, 258
Lonicera (honeysuckle) 222, 247, 248
Luzula sylvatica 92–3
Lychnis coronaria 193, *193*

Magnolia 77, 177
Marchant, Chris and Toby 137
Meconopsis cambrica 108, 138, 144, 176
Melianthus major 141–2, *141*, 238–9, 260
Milium effusum 'Aureum' 137, 142, 200
mind-your-own-business 35, 93
Miscanthus napalensis 58, *58*, 200
Molinia caerulea subsp. *arundinacea*
    'Transparent' 58, *63*, 91, *145*, 184, *185*, 200,
    230–1, 234–5
Molopospermum peloponnesiacum 140, *140*
Mossman, Frances 18, 50
mulch 34, 62, 90, 107–9
mycorrhizal fungi 159
myrtle 64, 178, 199, 257
Myrtus communis 64

Narcissus 92, 109–11, *109–11*, 122, 137, 232
Nasturtium 'Mahogany' 243, *243*, 246
Nectaroscordum 90, 123
Nerine bowdenii 170, 238–9, 245–6, 257
Nicotiana 96, 109, 243
    N. mutabilis 62
    N. suaveolens 77, 96, 159, 182
    N. sylvestris 96, 159

Oehme, Wolfgang 229
Oenothera biennis 179, 184, *190–1*
Oudolf, Piet 171

Paeonia 244, 247, 248
    P. delavayi 136, 137, 142, 244
    P. 'Late Windflower' 98, 127, 138, *150–1*
    P. mlokosewitschii 91, *91*, 137, *137*, 178

Panicum 58, 200
Papaver
    P. rupifragum 108, *176*
    P. somniferum (opium poppy) 92, 95, *101*, 109,
        123, 243, *243*
Paris 98, 139–40, *139*, 231
Parthenocissus 220, 221, *221*, 222, 257
paths 36, 37, 93
Peckham home 18–22
    garden clearance 34–5
    garden design 22–3, 34–7, 62–3
Pelargonium 23, 36, 158, *161*, 218–20, 260–61
    P. 'Mrs Pollock' 218–9, *218*
    P. 'Peppermint Lace' 219, *219*
    P. 'Purple Unique' 220, *220*
    P. 'Stadt Bern' *199*, *201*, 218
perennials
    control 123
    dividing 248
    ground cover 92–3
    potting-on 158
    pruning 91
    winter protection 259–61
Persicaria 90, 99, 124, 206–7, 228–30, *229–31*,
    234–5, 248
Phyllostachys 64, 159, 160, *160*, 169
planting
    bare-root plants 61
    enriching soil 60–1, 62
    finding right position 59–60, 61–2
    hierarchy 178
    transparancy 199–200, 217
Podophyllum hexandrum 139, 193
Polygonatum x *hybridum* 127, 143, *143*
poplars 247, 248
poppies
    see also Meconopsis; Papaver
    Californian 92, 95, 243
    Chinese celandine 138

Index

Fairy Wings 95
opium 92, 95, *101*, 109, 123, 243, *243*
Welsh 108, 138, 144
posies *68-9, 137, 177-9, 176*
Potentilla 'Gibson's Scarlet' 193, *193*
potting-on 158-9, *161*
prairie plants 61, 200
primulas, candelabra 60
propagation 50, 245, 246-8, *248, 249*, 257
see also self seeding plants
pelargonium 218
perennials 248
pruning 49, 80, 89-90, *118-19*, 124
Pulmonaria saccharata 'Leopard' *137*, 139, 142,
142, 197
Pumphrey, Mrs Frances 59-60

raised beds 36, 95, 144-153
Ranunculus ficaria 74, *80*, 93, 94-5, *94*
rocket 95, 153
Rodgersia 60, 142
roof garden 17-18, 22, 141
roses (*Rosa*) 154-8, 221, 248, 257
R. banksiae 'Lutea' 74, *152*, 156, *156*
R. 'Cooperi' 64, 142, 156-7, *156*, 198, 222
R. 'Mermaid' 19, 34-5, 155-6, 222
R. odorata 'Bengal Crimson' 157, *157*, 241
R. primula 155, *155*
R. x *odorata* 'Mutabilis' 142, *142*, 157-8, *157*,
164-5, 178, 230
Ruys, Mien 200

salad 37, 95, 144, *144*, *148-9*, 153, 241
Salix exigua see willows, coyote
Salvia
pineapple sage 180, 260
S. discolor 218, 260, *260*
S. greggii 219, *219*
S. guaranitica 124, 178, *179*, 180, *190-1*, 193, *196*

Sambucus 'Black Lace' 179, 248
Sanguisorba 'Tanna' 193, *202-3*
Sarcococca 64, *68-9*, 76, *76*, 257
scented plants 75-80
Schizophragma 221
seating areas 35, *134-5, 163, 167*, 252
secateurs 49-50, *80*, 91
seeds
saving 236-7, 243-4, *243*, 247
spring sowing 95-7
self seeding plants 58, 94, 100, 107-9, 138, 178,
193, 231, 243
Senecio 64
shade plants 92-3, 97-100, 127, 138, 142
shadows 112, 184
Smyrnium perfoliatum 108, 142
snowdrop *see Galanthus*
soil 22, 24
improving 33-4, 60-1, 159, 248
temperature 95
worm activity 34, 58
Solanum laxum 'Album' 223
Soleirolia 93
spring 102-71
bamboo 159-60, 169
bulbs *46-7*, 90, 93, 109-11, *120*, 121-2, 158,
231-2
control 123-4
epimedium 126-8
flowers 128, 137-40
foliage/greens 140-4
iris *168*, 169-71
light 112, 121
mulching 107-9
potting-on 158-9, *161*
roses 154-8
sowing seed 95-7
vegetables 144, *148-9*, 153-4
wisteria 124-5

staking 62, *123*, 123–4, 183, 241

Stipa 121, 178, *236–7*, 243

Stylophorum lasiocarpum 108, *132–3*, 138

summer 174–223

    climbers 220–3

    ecosystem 196–9

    hemerocallis 193–5

    lilies 180–3

    pelargonium 218–20

    posies *176*, 176–9

    rain *162–3*

    solstice 179–80

    transparency 199–200, 217

    zenith 183–4, *186–7*, 193

Symphytum ibericum 92–3

Tagetes 96, 180, *210–11*, 218, *218*, 241

Tellima grandiflora 'Purpurteppich' 93

terraces 19, 20, 35, 93, *162–3*

Tetrapanax papyrifer 'Rex' 141, *141*, 142, *204–5*

texture 140, 178, 199

Thalictrum 184, *184*, *190–1*

Thamnochortus insignis 245

tomatoes 96, 153, *240*, 241, 242

tools 40, *48*, 49–50

Trachelospermum jasminoides 77, 222

trees 37–40, 64, 73–4, 196

    autumn colour 257–8

    cuttings 248

    light and shade 112, *113*

    staking 62

Tricyrtis formosana 230, *230*, *254–5*

Trillium 92, 98, 138, *138*, 231, 248

Tulipa 121–2, *121*, *122*, 232

    T. sprengeri 91, 122, *122*, 178, 193

    T. sylvestris 120, 122, *176*

Valeriana officinalis *150–1*, 198

Vauxhall, gardens 17–18, 22, 141

vegetables 33, 144, *148–9*, 153–4, 241–2

Veratrum 92, 139, 241

Verbena bonariensis 107, 193, *214–15*, 217, 229

Veronicastrum virginicum 'Album' 197

Viburnum 197

Vinca minor 93

Viola labradorica 74, 94, *137*

Virginia creeper *254–5*, 257

Vitis 89, 220, 248

    V. coignetiae 89, 141, 221, 222, *222*, 256, 258

    V. 'Fragola' 89, *248*

water elements 36, *54–5*, *104–5*, *174–5*, 226–7

watering 40, 49

water lilies 36, 184

weeding 58, 107–9

wildlife 196–9, 232, 247

willow 248

    coyote 39, 141, 178, 179, 198, 217, 223

    weeping 22, 36, 37

Wilson, E.H. 180

winter 52–100

    clearing-up 90–2

    preparing for 259–61

    pruning 80, 89–90

    scented plants 75–80

Wisteria 124–5, 137, 197, 221

    pruning 89–90, *212–13*

    W. floribunda 'Alba' 90, 125, *125*, *146–7*

    W. sinensis 125

witch hazel 78–80, 177

worms 33, 34, 58

Zantedeschia aethiopica 184, *185*

Garden Plan

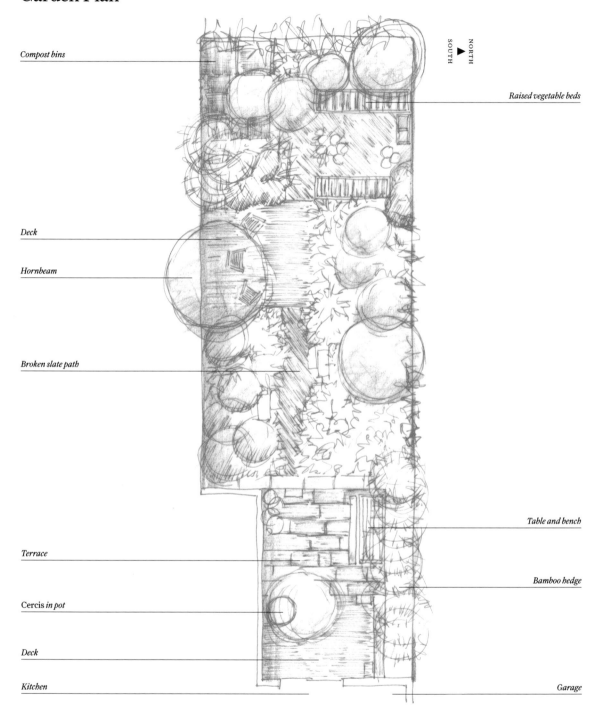

Compost bins

NORTH
SOUTH

Raised vegetable beds

Deck

Hornbeam

Broken slate path

Table and bench

Terrace

Bamboo hedge

Cercis *in pot*

Deck

Kitchen

Garage

Author's Acknowledgements

Thank you Huw, for your words of wisdom, your eye and being there so constantly as the sounding board. The process of making a garden is so much in the discussion, and making this place would not have been the same without you. The same can be said of this book.

Thank you Howard, for your evocative photographs and for understanding the garden so clearly. Your images capture the mood precisely but they have also revealed the garden anew through your impeccable eye. It has also been a pleasure talking plants along the way. I shall miss that. Thank you Allan Jenkins for teaming me up with Howard at *The Observer*. We have had a lot of fun along the way and it has never felt like work.

Thank you too, to family, friends and visiting strangers for your enthusiasm and enjoyment. Gardens are transformed through sharing. You have peopled and animated this place and given welcome and valued feedback.

Dominic, it has been good to know that, whilst we have been absent, you are a garden sitter par excellence and that both cats and garden are equally happy on our return.

The garden would also not be what it is without the raft of specialist nurseries that have helped to continually fuel my passion and have taken me so willingly on my diversions.

Thank you Anna Benn, for reading through the first draft of my manuscript and for your gentle, careful comments. It has also been a pleasure to work with Lorraine Dickey, Jonathan Christie and Sybella Marlow at Conran Octopus who, without fuss, have given me the space and support to turn thoughts into something you can hold and want to keep.

And, finally, well done Camilla, for finding us a garden with quite a nice house attached. It is a good place which has also provided sanctuary for numerous friends who came for a week and ended up staying months.

As this book goes to print it looks as though we will be parting ways with the garden and moving on. Whilst completing the final chapters, friends alerted us to a smallholding that was for sale on the other side of their stream in the West Country. I know that this is the right way forward, but it will not be easy to leave a place that has given me back easily as much as I have put in. It is time to look out rather than in and to explore another way of engaging with the natural world.

Dedication

For Boris and Eva,
who have a way of being there at just the right moment.

First published in 2011 by Conran Octopus Ltd,
a part of Octopus Publishing Group,
Endeavour House, 189 Shaftesbury Avenue, London WC2H 8JY
www.octopusbooks.co.uk

An Hachette UK Company
www.hachette.co.uk

Distributed in the United States and Canada by Hachette Book Group USA,
237 Park Avenue, New York, NY 10017 USA

Text copyright © Dan Pearson 2011
Special photography copyright © Howard Sooley 2011
Design and layout copyright © Conran Octopus 2011

The right of Dan Pearson to be identified as Author of this Work has been asserted
by him in accordance with the Copyright, Designs and Patents Act 1988.

All rights reserved. No part of this book may be reproduced, stored in a retrieval
system, or transmitted, in any form or by any means, electronic, electrostatic,
magnetic tape, mechanical, photocopying, recording or otherwise, without the
prior permission in writing of the Publisher.

British Library Cataloguing-in-Publication Data.
A catalogue record for this book is available from the British Library.

Publisher: Lorraine Dickey
Art Direction and Design: Jonathan Christie
Managing Editor: Sybella Marlow
Editor: Helen Ridge
Production Manager: Katherine Hockley

ISBN: 978 1 84091 537 2
Printed in China